Essential SQA EXAM PRACTICE

National 5 GEOGRAPHY

Practice Questions & Exam Papers

QUESTIONS & PAPERS

▶ Practise **50+ questions** covering every question type and topic

▶ Complete **2 practice papers** that mirror the real SQA exams

Sheena Williamson

HODDER GIBSON

AN HACHETTE UK COMPANY

The Publishers would like to thank the following for permission to reproduce copyright material:

Exam rubrics at the start of Section 1, Section 2 and Section 3 of both practice papers are reproduced by kind permission of SQA, Copyright © Scottish Qualifications Authority. Exam questions on pages 10 and 53 used with permission copyright © Scottish Qualifications Authority. No other content emanates from SQA exam material. Ordnance Survey maps on pages 2–3, 4–5, 6–7, 48–49, 50–51, 56–57, 64–65, 66–67 are reproduced by permission of Ordnance Survey on behalf of HMSO. © Crown copyright 2019. All rights reserved. Ordnance Survey Licence number 100047450.

Photo credits: p.21 © Shutterstock/Marharyta Kuzminova; p.23 © Shutterstock/Evgeny Sribnyjj; p.24 © Shutterstock/Sonia Dhankhar; p.34 © Shutterstock/M-SUR; p.35(t) © jcg_oida - stock.adobe.com; p.35(b) © Jeff Schmaltz, LANCE/EOSDIS Rapid Response/NASA; p.37 © Shutterstock/guentermanaus; p.38(t) © Shutterstock/Buffy1982; p.38(b) © Shutterstock/Ralf Geithe; p.54(tl) © Anirut Rassameesritrakool/123RF; p.54(tr) © Oleksandr Ivanchenko/Alamy Stock Photo; p.54(bl) © shootsphot/123RF; p.54(br) © John Morrison/Alamy Stock Photo; p.59 © Shutterstock/Domcontributor; p.71 © Pawel Bienkowski/Alamy Stock Photo; p.73 © COP21/Alamy Stock Photo.

Although every effort has been made to ensure that website addresses are correct at time of going to press, Hodder Gibson cannot be held responsible for the content of any website mentioned in this book. It is sometimes possible to find a relocated web page by typing in the address of the home page for a website in the URL window of your browser.

Hachette UK's policy is to use papers that are natural, renewable and recyclable products and made from wood grown in well-managed forests and other controlled sources. The logging and manufacturing processes are expected to conform to the environmental regulations of the country of origin.

Orders: please contact Bookpoint Ltd, 130 Park Drive, Milton Park, Abingdon, Oxon OX14 4SE. Telephone: (44) 01235 827827. Fax: (44) 01235 400401. Email education@bookpoint.co.uk. Lines are open from 9 a.m. to 5 p.m., Monday to Friday, with a 24-hour message answering service. Visit our website at www.hoddereducation.co.uk. If you have queries or questions that aren't about an order you can contact us at hoddergibson@hodder.co.uk.

© Sheena Williamson 2019

First published in 2019 by

Hodder Gibson, an imprint of Hodder Education

An Hachette UK Company

211 St Vincent Street

Glasgow, G2 5QY

Impression number	5	4	3	2	1
Year	2023	2022	2021	2020	2019

Cover photo ©

Illustrations by Aptara Inc.

Typeset in India by Aptara Inc.

Printed and bound by CPI Group (UK) Ltd, Croydon CR0 4YY

A catalogue record for this title is available from the British Library.

ISBN: 978 1 5104 7187 0

MIX
Paper from
responsible sources
FSC™ C104740
www.fsc.org

SCOTLAND
EXCEL

We are an approved supplier on the Scotland Excel framework.

Schools can find us on their procurement system as:

Hodder & Stoughton Limited t/a Hodder Gibson.

CONTENTS

National 5 Geography

The assessment of the National 5 Geography course will consist of two parts: a question paper (80 marks) and an assignment (20 marks). The two marks are added together to give a total out of 100. The question paper is therefore worth 80 per cent of the overall marks for the course assessment and the assignment is worth 20 per cent.

The assessment materials included in this book are designed to provide practice and to support revision for the National 5 Geography question paper.

The materials are provided in two sections:

1 Practice Questions   **2** Practice Papers

Together, the materials give overall and comprehensive coverage of the assessment of skills, knowledge and understanding needed to pass your National 5 Geography question paper.

Practice Questions

The Practice Questions are arranged into three sections to reflect the three sections of the question paper:

▶ Section 1: Physical environments

▶ Section 2: Human environments

▶ Section 3: Global issues

This section starts with a short commentary on the command words covered and question types you will find in the question paper. Each section is split into question types, and within each question type different specific questions are grouped together in How to answer features.

›› HOW TO ANSWER

For each specific question group, there is a short How to answer commentary which describes the type of question and gives some support in answering it.

Top Tips!

Top tips tell you how to improve your answer, give you suggestions about what the question asks, how to answer it and what to avoid in your answer. You will find these in How to answer features and alongside questions.

Practice Questions Key Area index grid

The Practice Questions grid on page vi shows the pattern of coverage across the three sections of the paper in terms of the question types, command words and OS map skills in the Practice Questions.

After having completed the questions in a question type section of the paper, you might want to use the check boxes to show progress. We suggest marking like this [–] if you are having difficulty (less than half marks), like this [+] if you have done further work and are more comfortable (more than half marks), and this [*] if you are confident you have learned a particular Question type (nearly full marks). Alternatively, you could traffic light them using colour – red for 'not understood'; orange for 'more work needed' and green for 'fully understood'. **If you continue to struggle with a question type, you should see your teacher for extra help.**

Practice Papers

Two Practice Papers are supplied in this book: Paper 1 and Paper 2. Each paper has been carefully assembled to be very similar to a typical National 5 Geography question paper. Each paper has 80 marks and is divided into three sections.

The question paper

The purpose of the question paper is to allow you to demonstrate the skills you have acquired and to show your knowledge and understanding from across the topics you have covered in the course. The question paper will give you the chance to show your ability to use mapping skills using OS maps; to extract, interpret and present numerical and graphical information as well as describe, explain and interpret information from the topics you have studied.

The question paper has three sections. In section 1, you will have a choice of question depending on the landscape type you have studied, and then you must answer all other questions. In section 2, you must answer all questions. In section 3, there are six questions and you must answer two from the six options.

Section 1: Physical environments

This section is worth 30 marks. You will have a choice of question depending on the landscape type you have studied, and then you must answer all other questions.

In this section, you can be asked questions on two key areas of **landscape types** and **weather**. You will have studied two landscape types, either glaciated uplands and coastal landscapes (normally question 1) or upland limestone landscapes and river and valley landscapes (normally question 2), with case studies related to Scotland and/or the UK. In section 1, there could be a physical question based on an OS map.

The question types you will meet in this section include skills questions, knowledge questions, and formation and weather questions. You might be asked to explain formations of features, for example corries, as well as explaining the processes involved in their formation. You may be asked to show the skills you have acquired throughout the course by assessing the suitability of a map area for a particular land use, for example recreation and tourism.

Section 2: Human environments

This section is worth 30 marks. You must answer all questions.

In this section, you can be asked questions on the three key areas of **contrasts in development**, **world population distribution and change**, and **issues in changing urban and rural landscapes**. Questions can relate to both developed and developing countries. The question types you will meet in this section are skills and knowledge questions. In this section, there could be a human question based on an OS map.

Section 3: Global issues

This section is worth 20 marks. In this section, you have a choice. You must answer two questions from a choice of six.

The six key areas on which you can answer questions are: **climate change**; **natural regions**; **environmental hazards**; **trade and globalisation**; **tourism**; and **health**. Each question has the same level of difficulty – no question is easier or more difficult than another. There are usually two parts to each question. Part A questions usually have a graph, diagram or map for you to describe in detail, using the information on it, and they are each worth 4 marks. Part B questions require a description, an explanation or assessment of the particular topic and are each worth 6 marks. In total each question (part A and B together) is worth 10 marks.

For more information on the key areas you will be assessed on in the exam, go to the SQA website and search for Geography (www.sqa.org.uk).

Timing

If you are attempting to complete a full question paper, you will need the full 2 hours 20 minutes. Try to allow yourself around 50 minutes to complete the **Physical environments** section, 50 minutes for the **Human environments** section and 30 minutes for the **Global issues** section. This will leave 10 minutes across the three sections for you to read the questions, make your choice of question in the Global issues section and to look over your answers at the end of the paper.

Practice Papers Key Area index grid

The key area index grid on pages vii–viii shows the pattern of coverage of the knowledge in the key areas and the skills across the two Practice Papers.

Using the Questions and Papers

We recommend working between attempting questions or papers and studying the answers.

Where any difficulty is encountered, it is worth trying to consolidate your knowledge and skills. If you have difficulty answering any questions, it is worth looking back at How to answer text and the Top tips, and also looking at marking schemes for similar questions.

You will need a **pen**, **sharp pencil**, **clear plastic ruler** and a **calculator** for the best results. A couple of **different coloured highlighters** could also be handy.

Answers

The answers to the Practice Questions and Practice Papers appear at the end of each of those sections respectively.

The answers to the questions in the Practice Papers include hints, to help you answer the questions. Do not feel you need to use them all! They focus on the geography itself as well providing tips and advice on the wording of answers and notes about commonly made errors.

Practice Questions

This grid shows the pattern of coverage across the three sections of the paper in terms of the question types, command words and OS map skills tested in the Practice Questions.

Section	Question Type	Command Words					OS Map Skills	Check
		Describe (in detail)	Explain (in detail)	Identify	Match	Measure		
Physical environments	Skills	Q2	Q8	Q1, Q6	Q3, Q4, Q5, Q7	Q7	Q1–8	☐
	Knowledge		Q9, Q10, Q11					☐
	Formation		Q12, Q13					☐
	Weather		Q14, Q16, Q18					☐
Human environments	Skills	Q3	Q1, 4		Q2		Q1–4	☐
	Knowledge	Q5, 6						☐
Global issues	Part A	Q1–12						☐
	Part B	Q18	Q13–17, Q19–24					☐
							Totals:	☐

Practice Papers

	Paper 1	Paper 2
PHYSICAL ENVIRONMENTS		
Ordnance Survey	Yes	Yes
Landscape types		
Identifying features	OS – Q1a, Q2a, Q3	OS – Q1a, Q2a
Formation of glacial features		Q1b
Formation of river features	Q2b	Q2b
Formation of coastal features	Q1b	
Landscape land use	Q4	OS – Q3, Q6
Land use conflicts	Q5	Q6
Weather		
Factors affecting local weather conditions		Q4
Synoptic chart – depressions and anticyclones	Q6	Q5
Anticyclones	Q7	Q5
HUMAN ENVIRONMENTS		
Ordnance Survey	Yes	Yes
Population		
Indicators of development	Q11a, Q11b	
Population distribution		Q9
Changes in birth and death rates		Q11
Urban		
Characteristics of land use zones	OS – Q8, Q9, Q10	OS – Q7a, Q8
Recent developments in land use zones		OS – Q7b
Shanty town improvements		Q10
Rural		
Modern developments in farming in developing countries	Q12	Q11
GLOBAL ISSUES		
Handling information		
Pie chart	Q13a	Q12a, Q15a
Map	Q15a, Q18a	Q14a, Q17a
Line graph	Q16a	
Bar graph	Q14a, Q17a	Q13a
Divided bar graph		Q16a
Climate change		
Managing climate change	Q13b	
Local and global effects of climate change		Q12b

	Paper 1	Paper 2
Impact of human activity on the natural environment		
Effects of human activity on the rainforest or tundra	Q14b	
Causes of land degradation in the rainforest		Q13b
Environmental hazards		
Strategies to reduce effects of hazard	Q15b	
Predicting and planning for an environmental hazard		Q14b
Trade and globalisation		
Inequalities in trade	Q16b	
Effects of changing demand for a product in a developing country		Q15b
Tourism		
Impact of mass tourism	Q17b	
Ecotourism		Q16b
Health		
Methods to control disease – AIDS	Q18b	
Causes of heart disease, cancer or asthma		Q17b

	Paper 1	Paper 2

Practice makes permanent

In this section, you will have the opportunity to practise the different question types that will appear in your question paper.

The Practice Questions are grouped first by area of study, and then by question type. There are three areas of study: Physical environments, Human environments and Global issues. Each question type is preceded by a How to answer section, which gives advice on how to answer that particular question type.

The command words used in the questions are also discussed throughout this section. The main command words that you will come across in your question paper are:

- ▶ describe/describe in detail
- ▶ explain
- ▶ identify
- ▶ match
- ▶ measure.

Question types

Skills questions

You will need to demonstrate geographical skills and techniques in the context of Physical environments and Human environments and Global Issues. Some of the skills questions in these areas of study are related to an Ordnance Survey map based on a landscape type you have studied in the UK.

Knowledge questions

You will need to apply detailed knowledge and understanding of the areas of study.

In Physical environments, you will be tested on your knowledge and understanding of the processes and interactions at work within physical environments across the two key areas of **landscapes** and **weather**.

In Human environments, you will be tested on your knowledge and understanding of the interactions at work within human environments across the three key areas of **population**, **urban areas** and **rural areas**.

In Global issues, you will be tested on your knowledge and understanding of six significant global geographical issues: **climate change**, **natural regions**, **environmental hazards**, **trade and globalisation**, **tourism** and **health**.

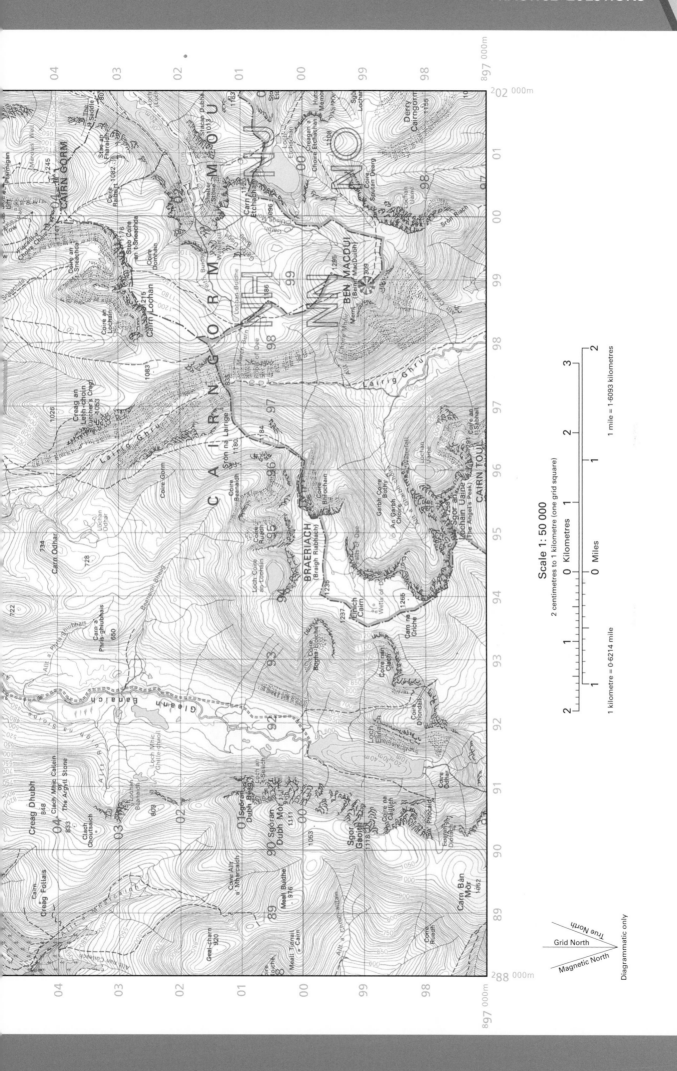

Scale 1: 50 000

2 centimetres to 1 kilometre (one grid square)

1 kilometre = 0·6214 mile

1 mile = 1·6093 kilometres

True North
Grid North
Magnetic North

Diagrammatic only

OS map showing Malham

For a detailed key, please refer to page 6.
Scale 1:50 000

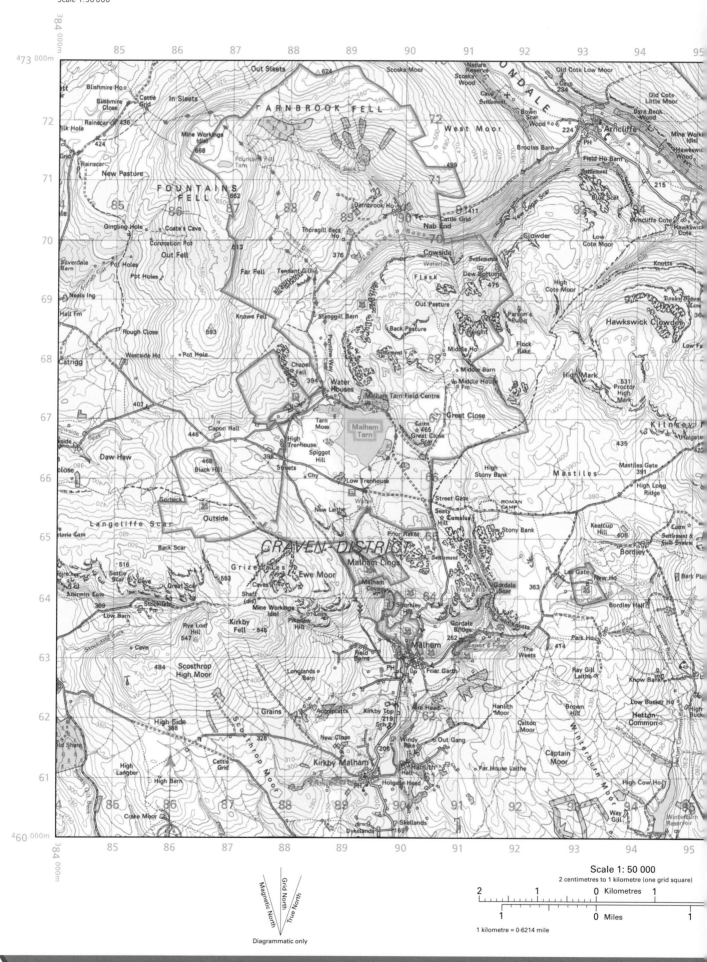

Scale 1: 50 000
2 centimetres to 1 kilometre (one grid square)

Kilometres

Miles

1 kilometre = 0·6214 mile

Magnetic North

Grid North

True North

Diagrammatic only

6093 kilometres

Ordnance Survey

OS map showing Oxford
Extract produced by Ordnance Survey 2018. © Crown copyright 2019.
All rights reserved. Ordnance Survey, OS, OS logos and Landranger are registered trademarks of OS, Britain's mapping agency.
Reproduction in whole or in part by any means is prohibited without the prior written permission of Ordnance Survey. **For educational use only.**

1:50 000 Scale
Landranger Series

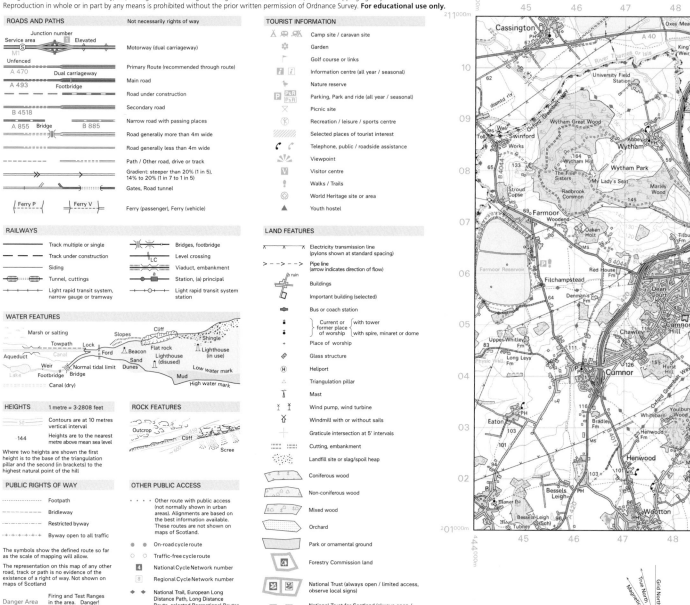

Extract No 2303/164

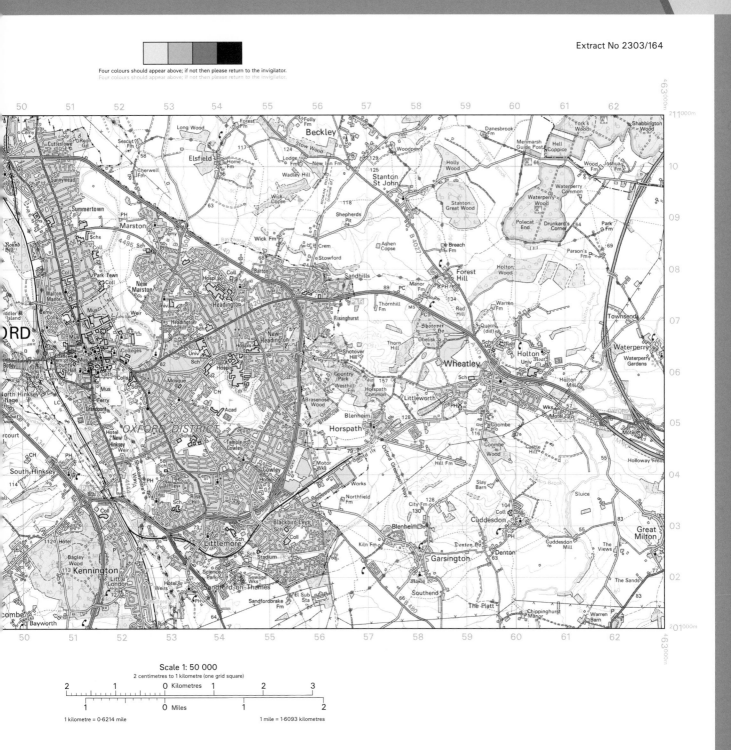

Scale 1: 50 000
2 centimetres to 1 kilometre (one grid square)

1 kilometre = 0·6214 mile   1 mile = 1·6093 kilometres

Section 1: Physical environments

Skills questions

There are skills questions in both the **landscape types** and **weather** key areas. There is no set number of marks for these questions and they can vary from paper to paper. Marks for each individual question can range from 3 to 6.

In the **landscape types**, there are four landscapes types and you will study **two** of them:

▶ glaciated uplands, and coastal landscapes

OR

▶ upland limestone, and rivers and their valleys.

Question 1 is normally based on glaciation uplands and/or coastal landscapes, while question 2 is normally based on upland limestone and/or rivers and their valleys. The two questions are similar in style and of equal demand.

You can choose between questions 1 and 2. You should only answer one of them, either question 1 or 2. Make sure you answer the question related to the landscapes you have studied.

Ordnance Survey map questions

In the **landscape types**, many of the skills questions are based on an Ordnance Survey (OS) map. These questions include command words which will indicate what you need to do in order to answer the question. The command words you will come across in questions in this section are 'describe', 'explain', 'identify' and 'match'.

The OS map questions could include instructions to:

▶ Describe features that identify a landscape type from an OS map.

▶ Identify features from an OS map using contour patterns.

▶ Match grid references to specific features on an OS map.

▶ Identify features from a diagram/cross section.

▶ Measure distances between places.

▶ Explain land use on an OS map.

Top Tip!

To gain the most marks from Ordnance Survey map questions six-figure grid references should be used.

Providing map evidence to identify a specific landscape

>> HOW TO ANSWER

Study the map carefully for a few minutes. Pay particular attention to the contour lines. If they are close together, this means the land is hilly/mountainous so could show a glaciated landscape. Next look for clues from the named places/features on the map. If there are words like 'coire', 'corrie' or 'lochan' this would indicate a glaciated landscape. Make note of where these words are found, as this is your map evidence to use in your answer.

To answer this type of question fully, map evidence should be given in the following ways. Give a grid reference and state the name of the feature, for example 'a corrie is found at 535275', or you can identify a feature and give its name, for example 'a corrie loch named Loch Fi'.

Questions on other landscape types should be answered in the same way.

Top Tip!

Avoid a general list of glaciated features or river features. This will gain you few marks as this is not map evidence.

1 Study the Ordnance Survey map of the Aviemore area.
   Give map evidence to identify that the map area has been glaciated.   4

2 Study the Ordnance Survey map extract of the Aviemore area.
   Describe the physical features of the River Druie and its valley between 917000 and 927050. You should use grid references in your answer.   4

Identifying features on an OS map

>> HOW TO ANSWER

Specific features on OS maps can be identified by the pattern of the contour lines or by matching features to grid references.

With contour pattern questions, start by looking at each of the diagrams. Match the ones you are sure of. Start with the easiest one first. On a glaciated map, this is usually a corrie as the contours are a distinctive armchair shape so it is easy to identify. If you are unsure about the rest, do not give up – apply your knowledge of contour lines to try to work out the rest of the answers. If you are still unsure then make a guess.

With matching grid reference questions, try the following. Start with the first grid reference, find the location on the map and then try to match it to one of the possibilities. Do the same with the other grid references to identify them all. Match the ones you know then guess the rest.

Top Tip!

Do not leave any feature unmatched. Match the ones left at random – you might be lucky and get it right!

MARKS

3

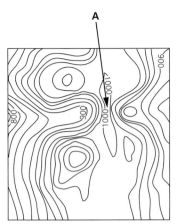 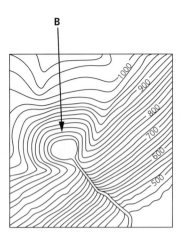 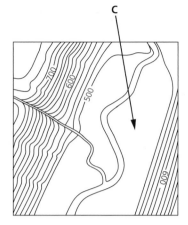

Diagram Q3: Glacial contour patterns

Look at Diagram Q3.

Match features A, B and C with the correct features below.

Choose from: pyramidal peak, U-shaped valley, corrie and arête.

> **Top Tip!**
>
> In this type of question, be aware that there is usually a distractor – an additional grid reference or feature which does not match anything in the question.

3

4 Study the Ordnance Survey map extract of the Aviemore area.

Match the glaciated upland features shown below with the correct grid reference.

Features: corrie, arête, U-shaped valley

Choose from grid references: 954976, 001981, 917005, 947005

3

5 Study the Ordnance Survey map extract of the Malham area.

Match the limestone features shown below with the correct grid reference.

Features: limestone pavement, intermittent drainage, pot hole

Choose from grid references: 894657, 900648, 861681, 853632

3

6

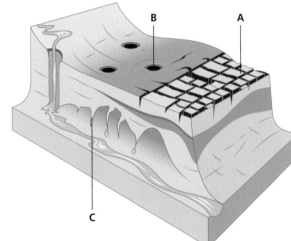

Diagram Q6: Limestone landscape

Study Diagram Q6.

Identify and name features A, B and C.

> **Top Tip!**
>
> This is basic knowledge. Make sure you learn to identify the features before you sit the question paper. A similar question could be asked about river features, coastal features or glaciated features.

3

Measuring distances on maps

➤➤ HOW TO ANSWER

The first step is to identify the scale of the map. This is shown at the bottom of the map. Maps used are either 1:25,000 or 1:50,000. Most maps used in the question paper are 1:50,000 which means that 2 cm = 1 km. Next take each measurement in turn. Find the two grid references on the map and mark each spot. Place the 0 line of your ruler on the first point then measure between the two points and note the distance. Whatever measurement you get, divide the answer by 2 to convert it to kilometres as the scale is 2 cm to 1 km.

MARKS

7 Study the Ordnance Survey map extract of the Oxford area.

Measure the three distances (A, B and C) between the places shown in the table.

Match your answers for A, B and C with the distances given below.

A	From the public telephone in Henwood (4702) to the school near Rose Hill (5303)
B	From Forest Farm (5410) to the church in Stanton St John (5709)
C	From Waterperry Gardens (6206) to the college (5502)

Choose from the following distances:

8 km, 6 km, 5.25 km, 3.75 km

3

Top Tip!

Practise this type of question to ensure you are familiar with measuring distances on a map. Read the scale at the bottom of the map!

Land use questions

These questions can be asked about the land uses in a particular landscape with or without reference to an OS map. This can include land use or land use conflicts and their solutions. The main land uses are farming, forestry, recreation/tourism, water storage/supply, industry and renewable energy. These questions usually have the command word 'explain'. This means you need to give a reason in your answer.

Different landscapes using an OS map

➤➤ HOW TO ANSWER

Take a minute to read the question and study the map. Next identify a land use. Then give map evidence to show why that land use is found in that particular location. Give grid references to identify the area you are talking about. If the question is worth 5 marks, try to give at least five reasons in your answer.

Top Tip!

Your answer must refer to map evidence. Giving an appropriate grid reference (preferably a six-figure grid reference) will gain you a mark.

8 Study the Ordnance Survey map extract of the Aviemore area.

The area of the map extract is popular with tourists.

Using map evidence, explain the attractions of the physical landscape for tourists.

5

Knowledge questions

Your knowledge and understanding are tested in both **landscape types** and **weather** key areas. The main command words used in these questions are:

▶ describe
▶ explain.

Questions can also be asked about the land uses in a particular landscape without reference to an OS map. This can include land use or land use conflicts and their solutions. These questions usually require you to explain, so follow the advice given in the two How to answer sections below.

Top Tip!

Do not list the type of activities that you identify on the map – this is simple description. For example, 'The area can be used to ski, climb, sail, and so on' is description. For explanation, you should say, 'There are mountains in the area which have steep slopes so are good for skiing.' Name the feature on the map, then give the reason why it attracts tourists.

Land use questions

➤➤ HOW TO ANSWER

Start your answer by stating at the beginning an area you have studied, for example for a glaciated landscape: the Lake District. Then write down the different ways that people use the landscape, and for each one say why that land use is appropriate for that area. For example, if you say people use it for recreation and tourism, state the features of the landscape that attract tourists: there are lakes which people can use for boating and fishing as well mountains that can be used for climbing.

Top Tip!

Make sure to learn the particular land uses associated with the landscapes you are studying. In your answer, always refer to a particular area you have studied and give some examples in your answer. Refer to a variety of different land uses.

9 Explain different ways in which people use upland limestone landscapes.

4

10 Explain different ways in which people use glaciated landscapes.

4

Land use conflicts and solutions

➤➤ HOW TO ANSWER

At the beginning of your answer, state the area you are talking about. Next state the two different land uses you are going to discuss, for example farmers and tourists. Next describe a problem, then explain why it causes conflict. Repeat this until you have covered six conflicts. If the question also asks for solutions, give a solution after each conflict.

11

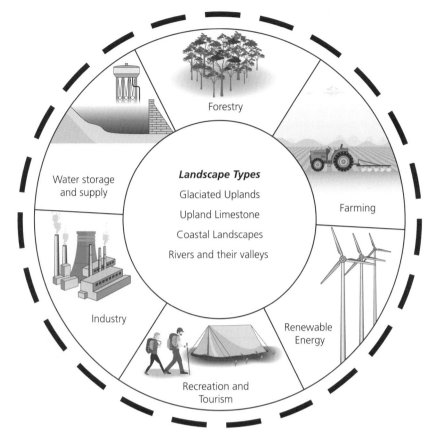

Diagram Q11: Landscape types and land uses

Look at Diagram Q11. For a named area you have studied, explain, in detail, ways in which **two** different land uses may conflict with each other and suggest ways that these conflicts might be reduced.

Formation questions

These are questions about the formation of a physical feature in relation to a particular landscape you have studied. To gain the most marks for this type of question, you should make reference to the processes involved in the formation of the physical feature. The more detail you put into an answer, the more marks you will gain. If you simply list the glacial processes like plucking, abrasion and freeze-thaw, you will gain only 1 mark. However, you will gain additional marks if you explain each of these processes. You can gain a mark for drawing a series of diagrams which show how the feature is formed at different stages. A diagram with labels which explains the formation of the physical feature can gain full marks.

Top Tip!

Make sure you name an area. Only discuss conflicts between two land uses. Explain what the actual problem is between the two land uses.

6

MARKS

The formation of a landscape feature

>> HOW TO ANSWER

Break your answer down into stages. Think of it as having a beginning, middle and an end. In the first stage, describe what it looked like and what caused it to develop. In the next stage, explain the main processes involved in its development and how the process affected the formation of the feature. In the last stage, explain the final look of the feature. In the case of a glaciated feature like a corrie, you should describe/explain the feature before, during and after the Ice Age. You should incorporate a sequence of diagrams in your answer. This will focus your thoughts and show logical progression in your answer.

12 Explain the formation of a U-shaped valley.
You may use a diagram(s) in your answer.

4

13 Explain the formation of a limestone pavement.
You may use a diagram(s) in your answer.

4

Weather questions

There are three main topics covered in weather. Questions can be asked on:

▶ the differences in local weather conditions in the UK

▶ types of air masses and their effects on the UK

▶ reading and interpreting weather maps, including depressions and anticyclones.

The main command words in weather questions are 'describe' and 'explain'.

Top Tip!

Do not just list the processes involved. You need to explain them. Only explain the feature asked for in the question. For example, if you are asked to explain a stack do not take it to the next stage and describe the stump, as this wastes time and will not gain you any marks.

The differences in local weather conditions in the UK

>> HOW TO ANSWER

Read the question carefully. The question gives you clues about what to put in your answer. Take each of the factors mentioned in the question and write at least a sentence about each of them. Remember you need to give a reason to explain how each factor affects local weather conditions.

MARKS

14

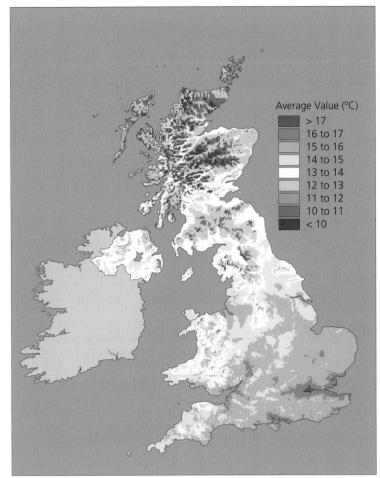

Diagram Q14: Average summer temperatures in the UK (Met Office)

Look at Diagram Q14.

Temperatures in London during the summer average around 17 °C whereas in the north of Scotland temperatures average around 10 °C.

Explain why factors like latitude, altitude, aspect and distance from the sea affect average UK temperatures.

Top Tip!

This question is about *average* temperatures, so do not talk about the weather brought about by depressions or anticyclones, which are not average but relate to specific days.

4

Weather brought by specific air masses

These questions are usually worth 3 or 4 marks. Read the question carefully as these questions can refer to different air masses and to different times of the year, which means they bring totally different weather. The questions may ask for just advantages, just disadvantages or both.

Describe how air mass affects the UK

≫ HOW TO ANSWER

First confirm the air mass and the time of the year you are being asked about in the question.

Describe the weather the air mass brings but do not stop there. Go on to state how that type of weather affects the people in a good way (advantages) then in a bad way (disadvantages). You should try to make at least five points.

15

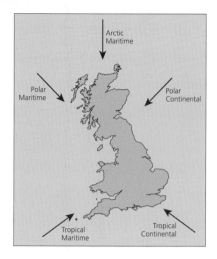

Diagram Q15: Air masses affecting the UK

Look at Diagram Q15.

Describe, in detail, the advantages and disadvantages of a tropical continental air mass affecting the UK in winter.

Top Tip!

This question can be asked for any of the air masses shown in Diagram Q15, so make sure you know the weather conditions brought by each of them.

16 Look at Diagram Q15.

Explain the problems that a polar continental air mass can bring to the people of the UK.

Top Tip!

Read the question carefully. It only asks for problems. Do not waste valuable time giving benefits as this will gain you no marks.

4

3

Weather maps

These questions are based on reading and interpreting weather maps and symbols. The questions can be based on depressions and anticyclones. They can relate to any time of year. The questions can also incorporate both knowledge of weather maps and the skills needed to interpret them.

Describing weather station circles

≫ HOW TO ANSWER

Take each weather element in turn and describe the weather shown. You should state the differences in your answer, not just the temperature, wind speed, and so on in each place.

Top Tip!

You need to compare the two weather station circles. Try to make a statement on each element shown on the weather station circle.

17 Study Diagram Q17.

Describe the differences in the weather conditions at Palermo and Rome.

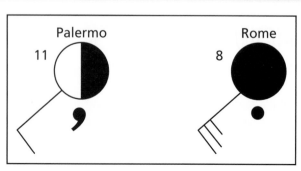

Diagram Q17: **Weather station circles**

3

Weather chart questions

➤➤ HOW TO ANSWER

Start off by reading the date and time of the chart. This is important as the weather associated with a depression, or more particularly an anticyclone, can be different in summer and winter. Spend some time studying the chart. Find the places on the map referred to in the question. Study each place and look carefully to see if there are weather fronts over it or close to it. Look at the isobars to see if they are close together or far apart. Identify if there is a depression or an anticyclone over the area which would explain particular weather. If there is a depression over the area, try to identify the stage of the depression that each town is in. Do not describe the weather in each place – you need to give reasons for the weather or differences in the weather in different places.

Top Tip!

It always rains on a front. Wind speed is always higher the closer together the isobars are. Another name for a depression is 'an area of low pressure' and an anticyclone is 'an area of high pressure'.

18

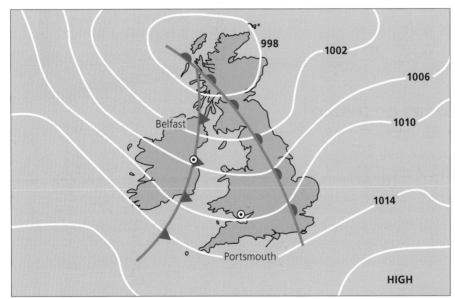

Diagram Q18: Synoptic chart for 26 February 2019

Study Diagram Q18.

Referring to the synoptic chart, explain why this has happened:

'The yachting competition setting out from Belfast has been cancelled but Portsmouth's will go ahead.'

(Facebook post)

Top Tip!

Look for the command word. Remember that in a depression the pressure is lowest at the centre, whereas in an anticyclone it is highest at the centre.

4

Section 2: Human environments

Skills questions

In this section, there is usually a skills question based on an Ordinance Survey map.

Ordnance Survey map questions

Many of the skills in the OS map questions in the Physical environments section are also found in the **Human environments section** OS map questions, so the advice is transferable from one area to the other. See the OS map questions in the Physical environments section for examples. The OS map would be an urban map with towns or cities on it.

In the OS map questions, the command words are similar to those in the landscape types key area of Physical environments, and include 'describe', 'identify' and 'match'. In general, OS map questions could include instructions to:

▶ Identify land use zones on an OS map.
▶ Identify features from an aerial photograph.
▶ Describe features that identify a particular land use zone.
▶ Match grid references to specific land use zones.
▶ Identify zones from a diagram/photo/cross section.
▶ Measure distances between places.

> **Top Tip!**
>
> In the Human environments section, you should be able to identify specific land use zones from a map and give map evidence as to how you identified them. You should be able to use map evidence to give advantages and disadvantages of the location of a feature, such as an industrial estate.

Identifying land use zones on a map

>> HOW TO ANSWER

Find the two areas using the grid references given. You will have knowledge of the type of features found in a CBD and the suburbs. Look at the map to identify specific examples found in this particular CBD. Then do the same for the suburbs. Do not give generic answers as not all features are found in each CBD or suburb. Try to give three examples for the two areas mentioned and give reasons to support your evidence.

MARKS

1 Study the Ordnance Survey map of the East Kilbride area on pages 66–67.

Give map evidence to explain why 6354 is the CBD and 6152 is the suburbs.

5

> **Top Tip!** In all OS questions, you need to look at the map and give evidence from it to support your answer. For example, do not simply describe a CBD from knowledge. You need to pick out the particular features shown on the map. If all the main roads meet at the CBD then give the number of the road, for example M74, so the examiner knows you have read and understood the map.

Matching land use zones

>> HOW TO ANSWER

Start with the first grid reference and try to match it to a zone. If you are happy with your decision, move on to the next grid reference. Continue doing the same until you have matched them all.

Top Tip!

If you are still not sure do not leave blank – make a guess!

2 Study the Ordnance Survey map extract of the East Kilbride area.

Match the grid references with the correct urban land use zone.

Grid references: 7155, 6452, 6954

Urban land use zones: CBD, new industry, new housing, old housing

3

Suitability of a particular location on a map for a development

>> HOW TO ANSWER

Find the proposed site on the map. Look at the area around the site not just the site itself. You should look for obvious things that are relevant to most sites. For example, look at the contour lines – is the site flat? If it is you can say that it is easier to use machinery on a flat site. Are there roads close by? If so then there are good transport links for goods and communications with customers. If there is a river close by, could it flood and destroy property/goods? Map evidence can be both good and bad if the question asks for advantages and disadvantages. Give named examples from the map to back up your evidence.

3

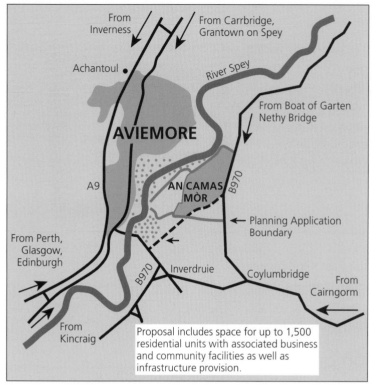

Diagram Q3: Proposed site of An Camas Mòr (GR903115)

Study the Ordnance Survey map extract of the Aviemore area (see pages 2–3) and Diagram Q3.

Find the site of An Camas Mòr at 903115. On the site at An Camas Mòr, it is proposed to build housing, businesses, community facilities and roads.

Using map evidence, describe the advantages and disadvantages of this proposal.

Top Tip!

You need to give both advantages and disadvantages to gain full marks. Put grid references into your answer as this can gain you a mark. Remember to use map evidence.

4 Study the Ordnance Survey map extract of the East Kilbride area (see pages 66–67).

There is new housing, found in grid square 6053.

Using map evidence, explain why new housing is found here.

Top Tip!

Remember the housing is already there so there is no need for negative points! In this question, you are looking for positive factors. For example, the A725 is close by so people can commute easily to work. Do not just say there is a road – you need to say why it is important.

5

5

Knowledge questions

There are knowledge questions in all three key areas of Human environments: Contrasts in development, World population distribution and change, and Issues in changing urban and rural landscapes. The questions relate to both developed and developing countries.

The knowledge questions in this section will usually include one of two command words:

▶ 'Describe' or 'describe in detail': say fully what the characteristics of a thing are.

▶ 'Explain' or 'explain in detail': give detailed reasons.

Questions on shanty towns

>> HOW TO ANSWER

Take time to read the question. Sometimes questions like this one require description and sometimes they require explanation. Always give a named example of a shanty town, for example Rocinha in Rio. If the question asks you to **describe**, then give lots of details. For example, residents continually upgrade their homes through a process of 'self-help' schemes, where the local people are provided with materials like bricks. If the question asks you to **explain**, state what was done and then say how it improved the shanty towns. For example, services have been improved, such as the provision of clean piped water (this is description) to help reduce the spread of diseases (this is explanation). The question is worth 6 marks so you need to make six points.

5

Diagram Q5: A shanty town

Look at Diagram Q5.

Describe, in detail, methods used by city authorities to improve living conditions in shanty towns. You should refer to a named developing world city you have studied.

Top Tip!

Do not simply list the improvements. Put some detail into your answer by giving examples from an area you have studied.

6

MARKS

6

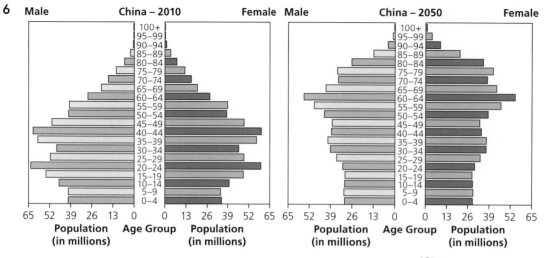

Diagram Q6: Population pyramids for China 2010 and 2050 (projected)

Study Diagram Q6.

Describe, in detail, the differences in population structure in China between 2010 and 2050 (projected).

3

Top Tip!

In this question, you must use figures and dates to gain full marks. Avoid describing one pyramid followed by the other. You need to make comparisons to get the marks. General statements like higher or lower/increasing or decreasing might only gain you 1 mark. Try to process the information in some way. You can be awarded a mark for overall trends.

7

Diagram Q7: Population growth

Look at Diagram Q7.

Explain ways in which developing countries try to control their population growth.

6

MARKS

8

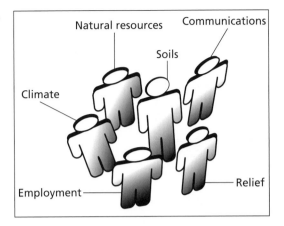

Natural resources
Communications
Soils
Climate
Relief
Employment

Diagram Q8: Some factors affecting population distribution

Look at Diagram Q8.

Choose three of the factors shown on the diagram. Explain how your chosen factors affect world population distribution. 6

> **Top Tip!**
> Do not list or describe the factors from the diagram. Take a factor and then explain how population distribution is affected. For example, deserts are too dry so this means that crops will not grow, so people will have a limited food supply.

9

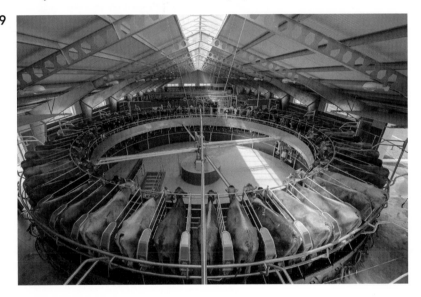

Diagram Q9A: Modern milking parlour

GM crops New technology Diversification Organic farming Government policy

Diagram Q9B: Selected farming developments

Look at Diagrams Q9A and Q9B.

Choose two developments from Diagram Q9B.

Explain how your chosen developments affect farmers in the developed world. 6

> **Top Tip!**
> Read the question – this kind of question could also be asked for a developing country, so be clear on what area of the world you are writing about. You need to talk about two developments. If you only talk about one development you will lose up to 2 marks.

10

Diagram Q10: Indian farmer collecting crops

Look at Diagram Q10.

Explain the advantages and disadvantages which modern developments in agriculture have brought to developing countries.

Top Tip!
You need to mention both advantages and disadvantages in your answer, otherwise you will lose marks.

6

Section 3: Global issues

There are six key areas in the Global issues section of the question paper: **climate change**, **natural regions**, **environmental hazards**, **trade and globalisation**, **tourism** and **health**. You will choose between the six key areas and answer questions on only **two** of them. Each of these questions is worth 10 marks.

The questions have two parts: part A and part B.

Part A questions are usually worth 4 marks and require you to describe, in detail, a graph, diagram, map or table.

Part B questions are usually worth 6 marks and require you to give a description or explanation that is specifically related to the key area.

The skills being examined in part A are extracting and interpreting numerical and graphical information, while knowledge is being examined in part B.

Command words

There are two main command words in the Global issues section:

▶ 'Describe' or 'describe in detail': If you are asked to describe in detail a graph, diagram, map, table or an event, then make statements containing facts. For example, if you were asked to describe the effects of a volcanic eruption, you could say buildings fell down, bridges were destroyed and the fields were flooded.

▶ 'Explain' or 'explain in detail': If you are asked to explain the effects of a volcanic eruption then you need to give reasons in your answer. For example, buildings fell down which destroyed cars and buried people beneath the rubble; bridges were destroyed which meant emergency vehicles could not get through to the injured people; or the fields were flooded so the crops were destroyed which affected the food supply to the area.

Part A questions

To gain maximum marks from part A you need to describe in detail. 'In detail' means that you need to use dates and figures or the names of specific countries in your answer. Avoid saying 'increase' or 'decrease' without referring to figures. If you are asked to describe changes, you need to give differences in your answer. Once you have mastered the skill of describing in detail, you will be able to answer any part A question.

In the case of pie charts and graphs, the answers are on the diagram. In the case of maps, the skill is identifying specific countries or areas. Part A questions should generally be linked in some way to one of the six key areas you have studied, but you should not require specific knowledge of the key area to answer these questions, as they will relate to a graph, diagram or map.

Part A questions are usually worth 4 marks. This means that you need to make at least four points to get 4 marks.

Questions based on pie charts

>> HOW TO ANSWER

Take time to understand the figures on the pie charts. Most of these questions are comparisons. Look at the same segment on each pie chart then use the information to show the differences between them. Subtract the figures, then write down the differences in your answer. Do the same with each segment in the pie chart. List at least four changes, preferably five to ensure you gain the full 4 marks.

MARKS

1

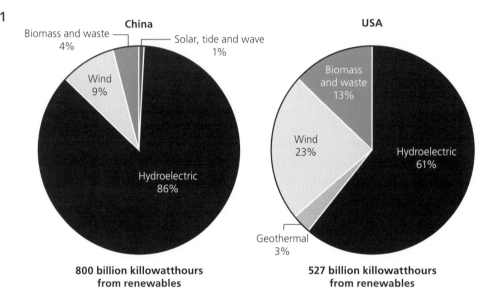

800 billion killowatthours from renewables

527 billion killowatthours from renewables

Diagram Q1: Renewable energy produced by China and the USA

Study Diagram Q1.

Describe, in detail, the differences between renewable energy produced by China and the USA.

4

Top Tip! In this and the next question, you must use figures to gain full marks. General statements where you have said that something is 'higher' or 'lower'/'increasing' or 'decreasing' might only gain you 2 marks. Do not describe China followed by the United States. The question asks for differences, so process the information you are given in some way to show this. For example, instead of saying China generates more renewable energy from hydroelectric sources (HEP) than the USA, you could say China generates 86 per cent of its renewable energy from HEP sources which is 25 per cent more than the USA.

2

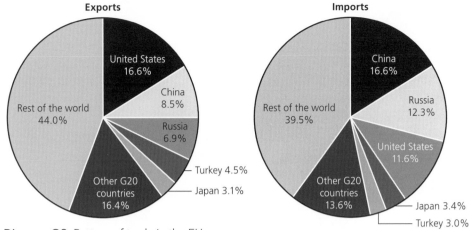

Diagram Q2: Pattern of trade in the EU

Study Diagram Q2.

Describe, in detail, the pattern of trade in the EU.

4

Questions based on maps

>> HOW TO ANSWER

First study the map to become familiar with the key. Then go through each category in the key and make a statement about it: identify two or three countries which fall into each category. If there is a recognisable pattern on the map then mention that in your answer. For example, on the map below, the continent of South America has the lowest carbon emissions per person in the world. Make at least four statements to gain 4 marks. If the question asks for a description of the distribution of earthquakes, then try to identify specific areas from the map, for example the west coast of the USA or the Pacific Ring of Fire.

3

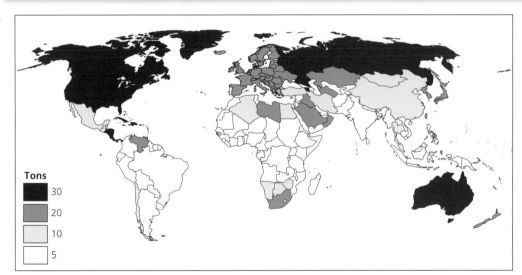

Diagram Q3: Tons of carbon emissions per person per annum

Study Diagram Q3.

Describe, in detail, the world distribution of carbon emissions per person per annum.

Top Tip!

Only 1 mark can be awarded for highest or lowest, so remember to use figures in your answer. You will only get 1 mark for each category, so only mention each category once.

4

MARKS

4

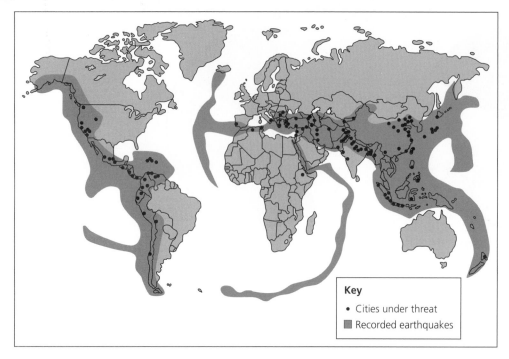

Diagram Q4: Cities under threat from earthquakes

Study Diagram Q4.

Describe, in detail, the distribution of cities most threatened by earthquakes.

Top Tip! A list of places might gain only 1 mark. Give a location, then name cities in those areas. Do not refer to areas where there are no earthquakes.

4

5

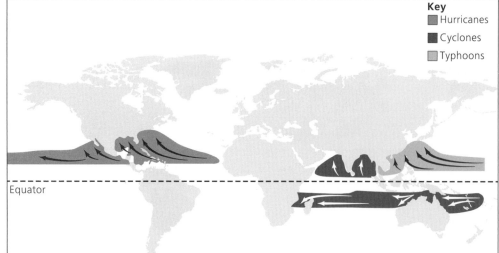

Diagram Q5: Location of tropical storms

Study Diagram Q5.

Describe, in detail, the distribution of tropical storms.

Top Tip!

Remember, the map is there to help you answer the question. Try to name areas or countries in your answer. There are no marks for explanation, only for description, so do not explain your answer. Do not list places as this will gain you only 1 mark.

4

MARKS

6

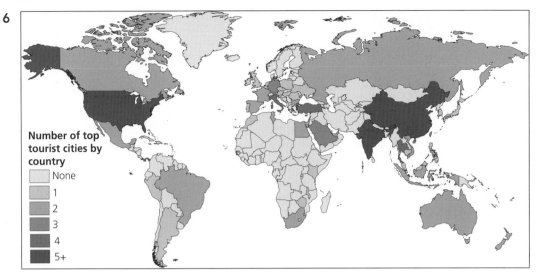

Diagram Q6: Number of top tourist cities by country

Study Diagram Q6.

Describe, in detail, the distribution of the top tourist cities by country.

Top Tip! Go through the key and try to identify countries associated with each category.

4

7

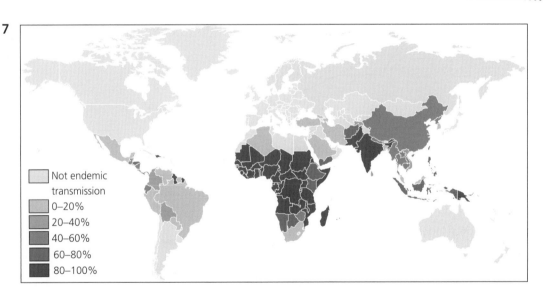

Diagram Q7: Percentage of population at risk from malaria

Study Diagram Q7.

Describe, in detail, the distribution of areas at risk from malaria.

Top Tip! Do not list places as this will gain you only 1 mark.

4

Questions based on line graphs

>> HOW TO ANSWER

Line graphs show changes over a period of time. If there is more than one graph then changes can be compared over the same period of time for more than one thing. Begin by reading the question to identify what you are being asked to do, then study the diagram to familiarise yourself with the scale/dates.

To get the marks from these types of questions, you need to use dates and numbers in each point to show differences or changes. Avoid simply giving a date then giving the amount for that year, for example: 'in 2007, 545,000 tons were produced' – this is not a difference so no marks would be given. Instead, for example, you should say: 'in 2007 there were 545,000 tons produced and this fell to 485,000 tons in 2008, which is a difference of 60,000 tons'. Try to identify a trend as this can also get you a mark.

8

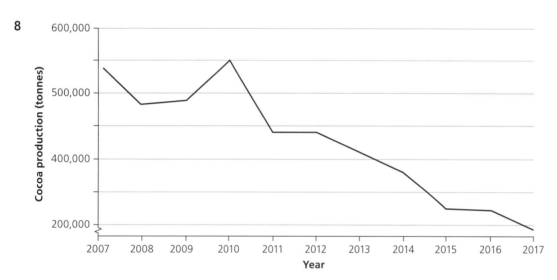

Diagram Q8: Cocoa production in Indonesia, 2007–2017

Study Diagram Q8.

Describe, in detail, the differences in cocoa production between 2007 and 2017.

Top Tip! Avoid simply saying increase or decrease. Use statistics in your answer. Line graphs show changes over a period of time.

4

MARKS

9

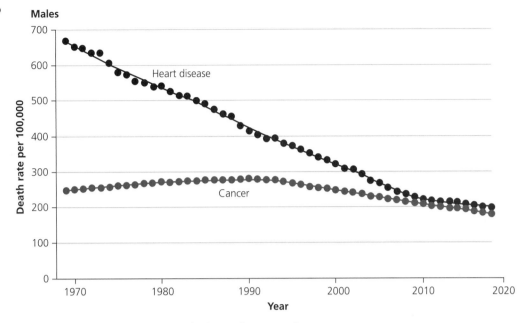

Diagram Q9: Death rates in males for heart disease and cancer

Describe, in detail, the changes in death rates in males for heart disease and cancer.

Top Tip! Both heart disease and cancer should be mentioned in your answer. You should use figures and dates in your answer.

4

Questions based on bar graphs

>> HOW TO ANSWER

Start by reading the question to identify what you are being asked to do. Study the scale. The advice is the same as above for line graphs.

10

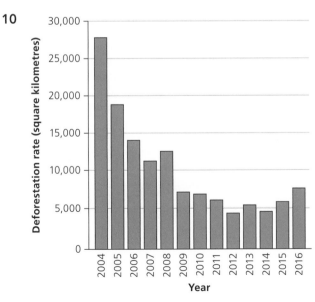

Diagram Q10: Deforestation rate in the Brazilian Amazon

Top Tip!

The question asks for change, so you must give a difference between two years in your answer. If you just describe each year and its amount you will not get any marks. You will get a mark for stating a trend.

Study Diagram Q10.

Describe, in detail, the changes in the deforestation rate of the Brazilian Amazon between 2004 and 2016.

4

Questions based on climate graphs

>> HOW TO ANSWER

In some key areas like natural regions, questions may involve a climate graph. These graphs show temperature as a line graph and rainfall as a bar graph on the same diagram. When describing the temperature graph, try to comment on the highest temperature, the lowest temperature with months and the range of temperature. Try to process the figures in some way. For example, the temperature in July was 16 °C which is 2 °C degrees higher than the temperature in May. Do the same with the rainfall, that is, mention months and the amount of rainfall. You can also identify trends, that is, say what months have had no rainfall or had the most rainfall. If you are asked to compare the climate of two areas you should follow the guidance above and compare the difference in temperature and rainfall between two places. For example, the highest temperature in Glasgow was 16 °C in July which is 1 °C higher than in Edinburgh.

Top Tip!

Temperature is a line graph and rainfall is a bar graph. If you mix these up you will not get any marks.

11

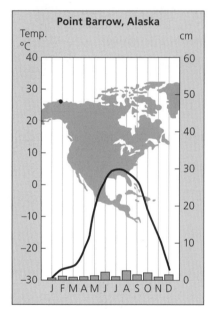

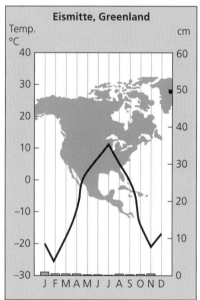

Diagram Q11: Climate graphs of Point Barrow, Alaska and Eismitte, Greenland

Study Diagram Q11.

Describe, in detail, the differences between the climate of Point Barrow and Eismitte.

Top Tip!

In this question, you must use figures and months to gain full marks. General statements involving 'higher'/'lower' or 'increasing'/ 'decreasing' might only gain you 1 mark. Try to process the information in some way. Marks can be awarded for overall trends. You must compare the graphs, not simply describe one and then the other.

4

Questions based on a table

>> HOW TO ANSWER

Read the question. Study the categories and figures in the table. Take each category then make a statement about it by comparing it to another category. Try to process the information in some way.

12

National Park	Visitors per year (millions)	Visitor days per year (millions)	Visitor spend per year (millions)
Brecon Beacons	4.15	5	£197
Cairngorms	1.5	3.1	£185
Lake District	16.4	24	£1,116
Dartmoor	2.4	3.1	£111

Diagram Q12: Visitor figures for selected UK National Parks

Study Diagram Q12.

Describe, in detail, the differences in visitor figures for selected UK National Parks.

4

Top Tip! In this question, you must use figures to gain full marks. General statements involving 'higher'/'lower' or 'increasing'/'decreasing' might only gain you 1 mark. Try to process the information in some way. Marks can be awarded for overall trends. Remember, you need to compare as the question asks for differences.

Part B questions

In part B the question commands are 'describe'/ 'describe in detail' or 'explain'/'explain in detail', although most are 'explain'. 'In detail' means that you need to use figures, examples and relevant information in your answer. 'Describe' means to give a detailed account, whereas 'explain' requires a reason in the answer. For example, if the question asks you to explain strategies used to reduce the impact of a tropical storm, a description would be 'board up the windows' but an explanation would be 'board up the windows because this prevents flying debris breaking the windows and people being injured by broken glass'.

The main types of question in this section are causes, effects and management strategies. Part B questions are usually worth 6 marks.

Top Tip!

In these questions, you are often asked to refer to a case study you have covered in your course. You should quote specific information relevant to your study. Avoid giving a general answer. For example, when discussing the effects of a volcanic eruption avoid saying 'hundreds of people died'; instead say 'in the 1980 Mount St Helens eruption 57 people died'. If you give a general answer, you may lose marks.

Cause questions

>> HOW TO ANSWER

In these questions, you need to give reasons why something has happened. Read the question carefully as these questions can be asked in different ways. For example, you could be asked to talk about human causes or physical causes or even both. Always refer to actual examples you have studied or give specific examples. Give a cause then say how it contributes to the event. You need to mention at least six causes to get 6 marks.

Top Tip!

A physical cause is something which occurs naturally, while a human cause has been brought about by human actions/interference.

13

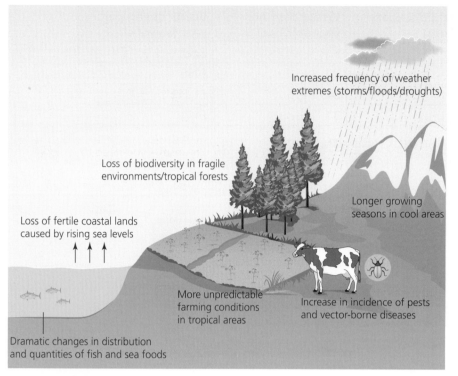

Increased frequency of weather extremes (storms/floods/droughts)

Loss of biodiversity in fragile environments/tropical forests

Longer growing seasons in cool areas

Loss of fertile coastal lands caused by rising sea levels

More unpredictable farming conditions in tropical areas

Increase in incidence of pests and vector-borne diseases

Dramatic changes in distribution and quantities of fish and sea foods

Diagram Q13: Some effects of climate change

Look at Diagram Q13.

Explain ways in which the activities of humans can cause climate change. In your answer, you should refer to examples you have studied.

6

Top Tip! Since these questions ask for detail or explanation you should avoid giving a list of points. A list does not have enough detail, and may not provide adequate explanation, and therefore will not get you all the marks available for the question.

14

Diagram Q14: Inequalities in trade

Top Tip!

You need to give reasons in your answer as the question asks for explanation. Try to mention specific examples.

Look at Diagram Q14.

Explain the reasons for inequalities in world trade between developed and developing countries.

6

15

Diagram Q15: Spanish beach

Look at Diagram Q15.
Explain the growth of mass tourism.

> **Top Tip!**
> Do not simply describe the growth of mass tourism – you need to explain why it happened. In your answer, use examples that you have studied. More detail equals more marks.

6

Effects/impacts questions

>> HOW TO ANSWER

If you are asked for a case study, start your answer by writing down the name of your case study. If the question asks for people and the environment, break your answer into two parts. Describe/explain the effects/impact on the people, then do the same for the environment.

16

Diagram Q16: Satellite image of Hurricane Patricia, 23 October 2015

Look at Diagram Q16.

> **Top Tip!**
> You should put as much detail into your answer as possible. You must refer to the effects on both people and the environment for full marks. You may lose a mark if you do not refer to examples of both people and environments you have studied in your answer. Try to talk about a specific tropical storm you have studied.

'Hurricane Patricia, with 200 mph winds, was stronger than the deadliest and costliest hurricanes in history.'

(National Hurricane Center, USA)

6

Explain the impact of a tropical storm on people and the environment. You must refer to named examples you have studied in your answer.

17

OVER
1.5 MILLION
FARMERS AND WORKERS
IN FAIRTRADE CERTIFIED
PRODUCER ORGANISATIONS

Diagram Q17: Fair trade

Look at Diagram Q17.

Explain the benefits fair trade brings to people in developing countries.

> ## Top Tip!
>
> The question asks for an explanation, so make sure you do not just describe the benefits. Say what the benefit is, then say why it helps the people, that is, give the reasons. Make sure you make enough points to gain 6 marks. Refer to specific examples you have studied as this adds detail to your answer.

6

18

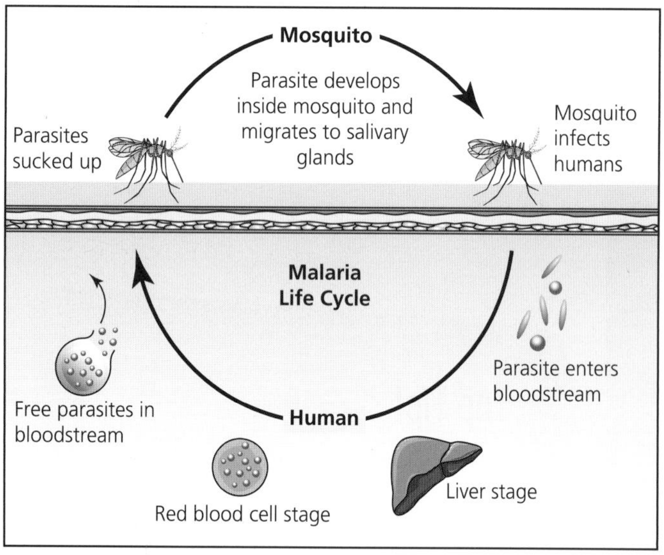

Diagram Q18: Life cycle of the mosquito

Look at Diagram Q18.

For malaria, cholera, kwashiorkor or pneumonia describe, in detail, the effects on people.

> ## Top Tip!
>
> Avoid listing. Although the question has the command word 'describe', it says 'in detail' so a simple list of effects will gain you only a few marks. You should put as much detail into your answer as possible. Try to refer to examples you have studied in your answer, such as particular outbreaks of the disease.

6

MARKS

19 Referring to examples you have studied, explain the advantages and disadvantages of removing tropical forests.

6

Top Tip! You should refer to specific case studies in your answer. Remember, the more detail there is in your answer, the more marks you can be given. A list of advantages and disadvantages will gain you only 1 or 2 marks. If you describe instead of explaining, you may get no marks at all. To gain full marks, you need to explain each of the advantages and disadvantages you have listed.

Management strategies questions

>> HOW TO ANSWER

Start by describing a strategy/method of managing the impact of a global issue, then say how it would reduce the effect/impact. Repeat this until you have made at least six points. In some questions, you may be asked to talk about a specific event like an earthquake. You must put examples from your case study in your answer and avoid giving general answers.

20 Explain ways in which climate change can be managed.

6

Top Tip! The command word in this question is 'explain', so you need to state the strategy then say why this reduces climate change. You can include strategies for both individual people and governments.

21

Diagram Q21: Rainforest destruction

Look at Diagram Q21.

Explain management strategies which can be used to reduce the impact of human activity on the rainforest. You should refer to examples you have studied in your answer.

Top Tip! Do not list the strategies. For each strategy, say what the strategy is, then give a reason for the strategy. Remember to refer to specific examples in your answer.

6

MARKS

22

Diagram Q22: Damage caused by an earthquake

Look at Diagram Q22.

Explain, in detail, the strategies used to reduce the impact of an earthquake.

You must refer to named examples you have studied in your answer.

6

23

Diagram Q23: Spanish hotel

Look at Diagram Q23.

For a named example you have studied, explain ways in which the impact of tourism can be managed.

6

24 Choose one disease from cancer or heart disease. For the disease you have chosen, explain the methods used to control it.

6

Section 1: Physical environments

Question	Expected answer	Mark
1	There is a corrie with lochan in squares 9400 and 0000 (1). There are scree slopes at 002978 (1). There is a U-shaped valley at 9100 (1). There is a ribbon lake at 9199 (1). There is a misfit stream at 915005 (1).	4
2	From point 917000 the river is flowing north (1) through a U-shaped valley in squares 9100 and 9101 (1). The valley narrows in square 9204 as the river flows through a V-shaped valley (1). The river is joined by tributaries like the Beanaidh Bheag at 924029 (1). There is a meander at 923038 (1).	4
3	A – arête; B – corrie; C – U-shaped valley	3
4	001981 – corrie; 947005 – arête; 917005 – U-shaped valley	3
5	894657 – intermittent drainage; 900648 – limestone pavement; 861681 – pot hole	3
6	A – limestone pavement; B – pot hole; C – stalactite	3
7	A – 6 km; B – 3.75 km; C – 8 km	3
8	The steep slopes have woodland on them, which can be used for forest walks and orienteering (1), for example the Glenmore Forest Park at 975109 (1). There are many rivers in the area like the River Luineag, which can be used for kayaking (1). Lochs like Loch Morlich can be used for fishing and boating (1). The steep mountain slopes can be used for rock climbing (1) and the corries and north-facing slopes can be used for skiing at 990060 (1). The beautiful scenery of the river valleys and the high mountains attract tourists (1).	5
9	In the Yorkshire Dales, tourists visit the area to see landscape features like limestone pavements and pot holes (1) around Malham Cove (1). The many caves in the area like White Scar caves attract tourists to see flowstone, stalactites and stalagmites (1). Abseiling down limestone scars is a popular activity (1). Many other activities such as caving, pot-holing, rock climbing and horse riding are also popular in limestone areas (1). Quarrying is an industry found in upland limestone areas (1). In the Yorkshire Dales, the main rocks quarried are carboniferous limestone, sandstone and gritstone (1). Cement works can also locate in limestone areas for the raw material lime (1). The upland areas can be used for sheep farming as sheep are hardy and can survive in the harsh weather conditions with poor grazing (1). Upland areas are suitable for generating wind power as they are higher up so more exposed to wind (1).	4
10	Upland glaciated areas like the Lake District tend to have a high rainfall which can fill the natural lakes and be used to supply water to nearby settlements (1) like Thirlmere reservoir which supplies many areas including Manchester (1). The hard, impermeable rocks are suitable for water storage as there is little loss through leakage (1). Natural features like hanging valleys allow fast-flowing water to be used in the generation of hydroelectric power (1). Upland glaciated areas tend to be quite windy so are suitable for the generation of electricity using wind turbines (1), e.g. Kirkby Moor near Barrow-in-Furness (1). Little can grow or survive on the steep slopes, but hill sheep farming is possible on the steep slopes as sheep are sure-footed and can survive in the harsh conditions (1). Forestry is possible on the lower slopes where the soil is less acidic and access is possible for the machinery used for logging the trees (1). Trees can also survive on the steeper slopes with poorer soil and can be used to stop soil erosion (1). These areas also attract tourists who come to see the dramatic glaciated mountain peaks and natural features like arêtes and corries (1) such as Helvellyn (1). The many lakes like Coniston Water can be used for water sports such as boating and sailing (1). The steep slopes can be used for hill walking and climbing, and in the winter the corries can be used for skiing and snowboarding (1).	4

Question	Expected answer	Mark
11	**Conflicts:** Tourists want to see the beautiful and unusual scenery of the Yorkshire Dales but quarries spoil the natural beauty of the landscape (1). Lorries used to remove stone endanger wildlife and put visitors off returning to the area (1). Large lorries needed to remove quarried stone cause air pollution and dust which spoils the atmosphere for tourists (1). Lorries cause traffic congestion on narrow country roads which slows traffic and delays drivers (1). Peace and quiet for visitors is disturbed by blasting of rock (1). **Solutions:** The quarries can be screened by trees to reduce the visual pollution (1). Blasting can be restricted to specific times, reducing the noise disturbance to tourists (1). The limestone can be moved by train instead of road, reducing congestion (1). The vehicles can be covered with tarpaulins to try to reduce the amount of dust in the atmosphere (1).	6
12	A glacier moves down a main valley which it erodes by plucking (1), where the ice freezes onto fragments of rock and pulls them away (1), and abrasion, where rock fragments embedded in the ice scrape the land surface (1). The weight and erosive power of the glacier remove interlocking spurs (1). As a result the valley becomes deeper, straighter and wider (1).	4
13	During the Ice Age, glaciers scraped away the soil leaving areas of bare limestone exposed (1). The limestone surface was then exposed to chemical weathering (1). Cracks appear in the rock as it dries out (1). Rainwater is a weak carbonic acid which reacts with the limestone as it passes through the rock (1). It dissolves the stone, enlarging the joints and bedding planes (1). The chemical weathering widens and deepens the cracks to form grykes (1). This leaves exposed blocks of limestone called clints, and the resulting pattern of blocks and spaces is called limestone pavement (1).	4
14	Areas around London have a higher temperature than further north as they are closer to the Equator (1) so they get more intense heating from the sun's rays as they are more concentrated (1). Urban areas like London, Glasgow and Edinburgh have slightly higher average temperatures due to the heat island effect (1). Places in northern Scotland are closer to the North Pole so have cooler average temperatures (1) as the sun's rays are less concentrated as they have more atmosphere to travel through (1). The higher up you go the colder it gets, so lower-lying areas like central Scotland are warmer than mountain areas like the north-west Highlands (1) because temperatures drop by 1 °C for every 100 metres in height (1). Areas which are south facing are warmer because they get more sun (1), while north-facing areas are colder because they experience cold northerly winds (1). Western coastal areas are warmer because of a warm ocean current called the North Atlantic Drift (1).	4
15	**Advantages:** People can take part in more outdoor activities such as swimming (1). Outdoor sports can take place, as well as tournaments like Wimbledon, without being rained off (1). School sports days can safely go ahead due to dry conditions (1). More people buy products like sunscreen and ice lollies and that increases shops' profits (1). Warm, dry and sunny weather makes people feel better (1). **Disadvantages:** There is a lack of water which results in hosepipe bans preventing people from watering their gardens or washing their cars (1). Drought conditions reduce the yield of farmers' crops (1). People suffer from sunburn and dehydration (1). More people are admitted to hospital with heatstroke (1), putting a strain on resources (1). Forest fires break out (1). Thunderstorms can build up in the afternoon causing heavy downpours and flooding (1).	4
16	More accidents due to the slippery conditions result in people being admitted to hospital with broken limbs, etc. (1). This puts an extra strain on the health service (1). Additional supplies of electricity are needed as people turn up their central heating to keep warm (1) putting pressure on the National Grid (1). Increased use of electricity means people have to find additional money to pay for higher bills (1). Freezing temperatures can cause pipes to burst leading to water damage to homes (1). Travel is disrupted, affecting business as workers cannot reach their employment (1).	3
17	In Palermo, the temperature is 3 degrees warmer than in Rome (1). The current weather in Palermo is drizzle while it is raining in Rome (1). Rome is much cloudier than Palermo by 4 oktas (1). The wind speed is higher in Rome than Palermo by 15 km per hour (1).	3

Question	Expected answer	Mark
18	There is a cold front close to Belfast causing cloud cover and wind (1). The isobars are closer together at Belfast so it will be experiencing stronger winds than Portsmouth (1). The front is over Belfast so it will be causing heavy rain (1). Portsmouth is in the warm sector so it will be drier and clearer (1). The isobars are further apart so it will be less windy (1). The cold front has still not reached Portsmouth so the weather is more pleasant, allowing the race to go ahead (1).	4

Section 2: Human environments

Question	Expected answer	Mark
1	6354 is the CBD as transport is easily accessed – there is both a bus station (1) and a train station (1). There are several churches found here (1). There is a Town Hall (1). 6152 is the suburbs as it is found on the outskirts of the town some distance from the CBD (1). The streets are more modern, with cul-de-sacs (1). There is more open space as well as an area of coniferous woodland (1). There are no main roads running through the area (1) but the A726 and the B764 are close by, allowing good access to the CBD and nearby town of Hamilton as well as the M74 (1).	5
2	6954 – new housing 7155 – CBD 6452 – new industry	3
3	**Advantages:** There is flat/gently sloping land for building on (1), it is built away from the flood plain so little risk of flooding (1). It is close to Aviemore so they will be able to access the amenities of the village, for example the railway station (1) at 895124 (1). There is a road close by, the B970, giving access to Coylumbridge and Aviemore (1). **Disadvantages:** Areas of forest would have to be cut down (1) destroying natural woodland and habitat for wildlife (1). Increase in traffic on the only road bridge across the river would lead to congestion (1). Electricity transmission line runs across the area so pylons would be an eyesore (1).	5
4	The land is flat so it is easier to build the houses on (1). The land on the rural/urban fringe is cheaper, so low-density housing with gardens/garages can be built (1). There is good road access nearby via the A726/A727/B764 (1) which people can use to commute to their work (1). The area is on the edge of the town, so there will be less noise and air pollution (1) and less traffic, so it will be safer for families (1). There are woods nearby, where residents can go for walks to relax (1). There is a train station with a park-and-ride scheme nearby which gives easy access to the town centre and Clarkston (1).	5
5	**If Kibera, Nairobi is chosen:** The shanty towns are being bulldozed over a period of time (1), and people are being rehoused nearby in newly built apartments (1). This housing is affordable for the people, and the new estates have facilities like schools and markets (1). New roads have been built, which gives more access to Kibera (1) and allows bin lorries to collect rubbish, improving the health of the people (1). Storm drains are being built to control flooding (1). Communal toilet blocks have been built to stop sewage contaminating the streets (1). Clean water is now available from communal taps so contaminated water no longer needs to be collected from the Nairobi Dam (1), reducing the spread of waterborne diseases such as cholera (1).	6
6	In 2010 there were about 152 million under the age of 10, but by 2050 this will be about 116 million (1). In 2010 there were very few over 80, but by 2050 there will be about 114 million (1). The number of young people will reduce by 2050 (1). In 2010 the largest age band was 20–24, but in 2050 it will be 60–64 (1). There will be fewer males in 2050 in the age group 0–4, dropping from 41 million to 30 million (1).	3

Question	Expected answer	Mark
7	China introduced a one child policy to help reduce growth (1). In 2015 China changed to a two child policy to help the gender imbalance (1). Benefits received from following this government policy could be taken away from families who did not follow this rule (1), for example less access to education, childcare and health care (1). China encouraged the use of birth control methods like sterilisation (1). Abortion is legal in China and is widely used (1). In recent years, China has provided more education on birth control (1). Some countries like Indonesia introduced more free contraception (1). In the Caribbean, sex education is being used (1). Countries like Russia use tax incentives to encourage smaller families (1).	6
8	Many people tend to live in areas where there are minerals and raw materials to extract and sell (1) as well as providing jobs giving a reasonable standard of living (1). Areas with good soil can grow crops providing food for the population (1). Some areas are isolated so it is difficult to access or export goods (1). Areas like the Sahara Desert are too dry to allow crops to grow so they support a limited population (1). In the tundra areas of North America, the short growing season prevents the growth of crops, so food has to be flown in, making it expensive to live there (1). Rainforests have a low population density as they are uncomfortable to live in due to the humid climate (1), and diseases like malaria spread easily (1). People avoid living in mountainous areas like the Himalayas as they are difficult to access (1) and difficult to build on as machinery cannot be used (1).	6
9	**If new technology is chosen:** Machinery increases the efficiency on a farm, enabling the farmer to plough, sow, spray, etc., more quickly, covering larger areas (1). It also speeds up harvesting and results in the product being delivered to markets fresher (1) and at a higher premium (1). It also allows for a smaller workforce and therefore lower wage bills (1). It allows for the use of satellite technology/computers to control the application of fertilisers to particular areas of fields, improving yields (1). **If diversification is chosen:** Farmers can obtain additional income from a variety of sources if they diversify their activities on the farm (1). They may turn old farm workers' cottages into holiday chalets, or use part of the land for a golf course, and they may earn income from sports such as quad-bike riding (2). If crop yields are poor, then farmers have another source of income to fall back on (1).	6
10	**Advantages:** The introduction of GM crops can give the farmer a more reliable harvest as the seeds are designed to resist disease (1). Crops can be grown in adverse conditions, for example lack of water, ensuring a better food supply for the people (1). The increased demand for biofuels can result in higher crop prices, improving the farmer's income, and can lead to more jobs (1). Mechanisation means less work for the farmer and it is quicker and more efficient (1). The use of fertilisers and pesticides increases crop yield (1), which leads to increased profit for the farmer (1), and this can increase their standard of living (1). Increased yields allow a surplus to be produced, which encourages trade to take place (1). **Disadvantages:** Mechanisation can result in unemployment as machines do the work previously done by humans (1). Machinery is expensive and not all farmers can afford it, so they find it difficult to compete with those that have it (1). Increased use of fertilisers and pesticides can damage the environment if they get into the water (1). GM seeds do not always taste good (1).	6

Section 3: Global issues

Question	Expected answer	Mark
1	China generates 86% of its renewable energy from HEP which is 25% more than the USA (1). China produces 1% of its renewable energy from solar, tide and wave power whereas the USA produces none (1). The USA produces 23% of its renewable energy from wind power compared to China at 9% (1), a difference of 14% (1). China produces none from geothermal power while the USA produces 3% (1). China produces only 4% from biomass and waste which is 9% less than the USA (1).	4

Question	Expected answer	Mark
2	The EU exports a larger percentage of goods to the rest of the world than it imports (1), the difference being 4.5% (1). It exports 5% more than it imports from the USA (1). It has a trade deficit with Russia (1), exporting 6.9% but importing 12.3%, a difference of 5.4% (1). It exports less to China than it imports by 8.1% (1). There is a very small difference in its exports and imports to Japan with 0.3% more imports (1).	4
3	Developed countries have far greater carbon emissions than developing countries (1). The areas with the highest emissions are the USA, Canada, Australia and Russia with most parts having 30 tons per person (1). The continents with least carbon emissions are South America and Africa with fewer than 5 tons per person (1). Only two countries in South America have emissions greater than 5 tons, and they are Chile and Venezuela (1). South Africa, Libya and Saudi Arabia have emissions of 20 tons per person (1).	4
4	Most cities are located on or near plate boundaries (1) where seismic activity is highest (1). Most earthquake threatened cities are found in developing countries (1) like Haiti (1). A large number of threatened cities are found in China (1). Three cities in Africa are at risk (1). All threatened cities in the USA are found on the west coast (1) especially along the San Andreas fault line (1) with a cluster around San Francisco/Los Angeles (1). There are many threatened cities around the Ring of Fire like Tokyo (1).	4
5	Hurricanes occur in the Caribbean in areas such as Jamaica (1). They also occur along the south-east coast of the USA affecting areas such as Florida and Mexico (1). They move generally in a westerly direction (1). Cyclones occur in an area stretching from Oceania to the south-east coast of Africa (1). Typhoons are found in South East Asia, stretching across the Indian Ocean to coastal India and Bangladesh (1).	4
6	The countries with over five of the top tourist cities are the USA, India and China (1). The state of Alaska has over five (1). The UK, Ukraine and Poland have one city (1). Italy, Germany and Saudi Arabia have four cities (1). In Africa, Egypt, South Africa and Tunisia have two cities (1).	4
7	Most of Africa south of the Sahara has over 80% risk of malaria (1) including Sahel countries like Sierra Leone and Chad (1). Only two countries in Africa have under 20%, South Africa and Algeria (1). Egypt, Libya and Tunisia are not endemic areas (1). In South America, only two countries have over 80% risk, Guyana and French Guiana (1). Brazil, Peru and Venezuela have less than 20% risk (1). The whole of India and Pakistan has over 80% risk (1).	4
8	In general, Indonesian cocoa production decreased from 2007 to 2017 (1), from 540,000 metric tons (mt) to 199,000 mt, a drop of 341,000 mt (1). It decreased from 2007 to 2008 dropping by 60,000 mt (1). It then rose from 480,000 mt in 2008 to 550,000 mt in 2010 (1). There was a large drop between 2010 and 2011, falling from 550,000 mt to 440,000 mt (1). From 2011 to 2017, it continued to fall, reaching its lowest point at 199,000 mt in 2017, a difference of 241,000 mt (1).	4
9	For both heart disease and cancer, the death rate has decreased (1). For heart disease, the death rate dropped from 680 per 100,000 in 1970 to 200 per 100,000 in 2019 (1), a difference of 480 per 100,000 (1). For cancer, the death rate per 100,000 was 250 in 1970 and this dropped to 190 per 100,000 in 2019 (1), a drop of 60 per 100,000 (1). Between 2010 and 2019, the number of deaths from heart disease levelled out, dropping by around 10 per 100,000 (1).	4
10	Overall the land lost to deforestation decreased between 2004 and 2016 (1) going down from 27,500 sq km to 7,500 sq km in 2016 (1). Deforestation reduced by 20,000 sq km in the 12 years from 2004 to 2016 (1). It decreased by just under 50% between 2004 and 2006 (1). It increased by 1,500 sq km between 2007 and 2008 (1). It decreased from then until 2012, dropping by around 8,000 sq km (1). It then increased by 3,500 sq km between 2012 and 2016 (1).	4
11	Eismitte's highest temperature is 7 °C more than Point Barrow's in July (1). The lowest temperature in Point Barrow is –29 °C in January compared to Eismitte at –27 °C in February (1), a difference of 2 °C (1). The range in temperature in Point Barrow is 34 °C as opposed to 36 °C in Eismitte (1). Point Barrow has precipitation throughout the year, totalling 13 cm, whereas there is less rainfall in Eismitte at around 9 cm (1). Rainfall is lowest in the months of May, June and July in Eismitte, whereas it is highest in Point Barrow in June and August (1).	4

Question	Expected answer	Mark
12	The park with the highest number of visitors a year, visitor days a year and visitor spend a year is the Lake District (1). The Lake District has 14 million more visitors a year than Dartmoor (1) and has nearly eight times as many visitor days (1). It has more than ten times the income of Dartmoor (1). The Cairngorms has only a third of the visitors a year that the Brecon Beacons gets (1) but earns just £12 million less (1). Dartmoor has more visitors per year than the Cairngorms but earns £74 million less (1).	4
13	People generate large amounts of waste, including plastic, which remain in the environment for many years and release gases which contribute to greenhouse gases (1). The production of electricity from fossil fuels like coal is responsible for the emission of huge amounts of greenhouse gases and other pollutants in the atmosphere (1). Inappropriate disposal of items like fridges releases CFC gases into the atmosphere (1). Increased use of timber for housing, for example, leads to the removal of huge numbers of trees which means that carbon is no longer absorbed by the trees (1) but is instead trapped in the atmosphere, leading to global warming (1). Population is growing in many parts of the world so more food is needed, leading to an increase in the amount of fertilisers used (1), increasing the amount of nitrous oxide in the atmosphere (1). Fumes from transport such as buses and cars release toxic gases into the atmosphere (1).	6
14	Developing countries mainly trade in primary products so receive less income in return (1) while developed countries like the UK have the technology to manufacture goods which produce a higher income making them richer (1). Many countries in Africa rely on exporting only a few products and so their economies are at risk from price changes and market demand (2) – if crops fail they have nothing to trade and they make little profit (1). They find themselves in debt and are forced to borrow money (1). They then have to borrow more money to pay the interest on the loans, further limiting their chances of development (1). Some countries have limited access to education, resulting in an unskilled workforce (1). Some countries are in trade alliances like the EU, which create barriers to trade for non-members (1).	6
15	There is a wide range of ways to travel as a tourist and these methods are widely available (1), for example car, boat and airplane (1). Areas are better connected by roads and motorways so are more accessible (1). The growth of budget airlines such as easyJet and Ryanair has brought prices down and increased the number of people who are able to travel (1). Holiday entitlement in many countries has increased over the past century which means that people can take more holidays during the year (1). In many families, both parents work so they have more money available to spend on holidays (1). The average family size has decreased, making holidays more affordable to more people (1). Package holidays are cheaper, so they are more accessible to more people, encouraging large numbers of people to travel (1). Holiday programmes and advertising have encouraged people to travel (1).	6
16	Hurricane Dennis caused widespread flooding along the Gulf Coast of America and the Barrier Islands (1) forcing people to leave their homes and seek shelter further inland (1). Homes and property were destroyed by the high winds and torrential rainfall, leaving people homeless (1). Several people died and many were injured (1). Farmland, power lines and bridges were destroyed (1). Protected turtle nests on Marco Island beach were destroyed (1). Roads were blocked with fallen trees causing disruption on the evacuation routes (1).	6
17	Fair trade ensures the farmer a living wage (1). More money goes directly to the farmer, as it cuts out the intermediaries who skim off some of the profits (1). Farmers receive a guaranteed minimum price so they are not affected as much by price fluctuations (1) and can receive some money in advance so they do not run short (1). More of the money goes to the communities and they can invest it in improving their living conditions (1). Money can be used to provide electricity and drinking water or pay for education (1). Fair trade also encourages farmers to treat their workers well and to look after the environment (1). Often fair trade farmers are also organic farmers who do not use chemicals on their crops and so protect the environment (1). Health-care services and education programmes are available and tackle the problems of HIV/AIDS (1).	6

Question	Expected answer	Mark
18	**If malaria is chosen:** Malaria is the second-biggest cause of death from infectious disease in African countries like Uganda and Nigeria (1). Ten million days of school are missed each year in Africa because of malaria (1). This leads to life-long learning disabilities (1). Expectant mothers are vulnerable to malaria. Risks to mothers and babies include low birth weight, miscarriage and maternal death (1). Malaria can cost families up to 25% of their annual income (1) meaning parents might have to choose between treatment and food (1). People cannot work so become even poorer (1). Malaria decreases gross domestic product in countries with high disease rates (1). **If cholera is chosen:** Cholera can cause extreme sickness, vomiting, muscle cramps and severe watery diarrhoea within two to five days of infection (1). This causes people to become dehydrated due to loss of body fluids (1), which can lead to shock, a severe drop in blood pressure and death if not treated quickly (1). Cholera often has the worst impact in areas where lots of people are living close together in insanitary conditions because the bacteria can spread so quickly from person to person (1). Cholera outbreaks tend to affect large numbers of people, especially children, who can die within 24 to 48 hours if they do not receive the right treatment (1). The impact on communities is therefore very high as workers are off sick and productivity is consequently very low (1). Families face hardship as a result of paying for hospital stays and medicines used to treat cholera (1). Countries face economic losses from the lost productivity of the caregivers (1); this affects the whole economy of the country as resources are used up fighting the cholera outbreak instead of being invested in other areas such as education (1).	6
19	**Advantages:** In Brazil large areas have been cleared by timber companies and the hardwood has been exported abroad increasing trade (1). Brazil is a poor country and this is a way of earning money for the country (1). Forests have been cleared to make room for new farmland to increase food production (1). The land made available by removing the forest can be used for settlement for the expanding population (1). Forests are also destroyed for mineral extraction. The minerals are sold to other countries and provide employment for some local people (1). **Disadvantages:** The habitats of wildlife are destroyed (1). Burning trees release vast quantities of carbon dioxide into the atmosphere and may contribute to global warming (1). The homes of indigenous tribes are destroyed (1) as is their traditional culture and way of life (1). Plants which may contain cures for diseases are also destroyed (1). Poor farmers lose their land and may be forced to migrate to towns and cities to find employment (1). This increases the number of shanty towns (1).	6
20	Many nations, including the UK, sign up to climate initiatives like the Paris Agreement (2015), where countries agree to try to take measures to limit global warming (1). In the UK, the government encourages people to make their houses more energy efficient by giving grants for things like solar panels, loft insulation, cavity wall insulation and double glazing, which reduce the amount of energy used (1). People can use public transport, ride a bike, and car share to reduce the number of vehicles on the road (1) or change to an electric or hybrid vehicle, so reducing the amount of exhaust emissions building up in the atmosphere (1). The use of fossil fuels such as coal, oil and natural gases can be reduced by introducing environmentally friendly fuels such as hydroelectric power, wind power, solar power and other renewable energy sources (1). Laws can be introduced to reduce the burning of forests so less CO_2 is released into the atmosphere (1). Replanting schemes can be introduced to replace trees where forests have been destroyed as trees store carbon and release oxygen into the atmosphere (1). Turning off lights, electrical appliances and turning down thermostats reduces the amount of fossil fuels used putting less CO_2 into the atmosphere (1).	6

Question	Expected answer	Mark
21	Some areas of forest are protected by being made into national parks, for example the Sierra del Divisor National Park in Peru (1). Laws are passed and rangers are employed to try to stop illegal logging, reducing the amount of forest lost (1). Clear felling large tracts of forest can be avoided to protect animal and plant habitat (1). Sustainable timber removal can be encouraged as this protects the environment but still makes money for the country (1). Areas can be replanted with fast-growing trees to establish a canopy to protect the forest floor from soil erosion (1). Publicity campaigns can be used to raise awareness of the problems (1), for example environmental groups like Greenpeace use demonstrations to try to influence government decisions (1). Developing countries should be paid a reasonable price for their timber to reduce the need to cut down trees to make money (1). The indigenous people should be involved in the protection of the forest as they have a vested interest in protecting both it and its wildlife (1).	6
22	People living in earthquake prone areas have emergency plans in place, and emergency supplies such as bottled water and tinned food are stockpiled to ensure they have vital supplies to survive in the event of an earthquake (2). In the event of an earthquake, short-term aid in the form of food, medicine and shelter is sent to the area to treat the injured (1). In Japan, people take part in earthquake drills to practise what to do in the event of an earthquake (1) giving them a better chance of survival (1). The government warn people, using text messages and TV, giving them the chance to move to a safer place (1). Earthquake-resistant buildings reduce the number of people trapped or killed (1). Sprinkler systems and gas cut-off valves prevent fires spreading, reducing the number of people injured and buildings destroyed (1).	6
23	In Benidorm, some hotels have energy-saving devices, for example all the room lights automatically switch off on leaving (1) and street lighting is low energy to reduce the amount of energy used (1). Tourists increase the demand for already scarce water supplies, so many of the taps are foot-pump operated to save water (1). Much food is sourced locally, reducing the need for transport and thus reducing air pollution (1) as well as the carbon footprint (1). Tourists are encouraged to put litter in bins to keep the resort and beach clean (1), and to shower before leaving the beach to reduce beach erosion (1). Promenades with shops and bars close by encourage tourists to walk rather than drive, which reduces air pollution and traffic congestion (1). Recycling bins are placed all around the resort, encouraging tourists to recycle plastic bottles, paper, etc. (1). In other areas like Mallorca, the Balearics' government introduced a tourism tax of around 1 to 2 euros a day to help preserve the island's environment threatened by increased tourism (1). They also have limited the amount of accommodation available to rent, thus reducing the tourist numbers arriving on the island (1). By-laws are in place in some resorts, which means all live music stops at midnight, reducing the impact on the local people (1). The government is encouraging tourists to stay in rural areas, for example in Pollensa Old Town, to reduce pressure on the coastal area of Puerto Pollensa (1), and it is trying to limit the amount of development allowed along the coast to protect delicate coastal areas (1).	6

Question	Expected answer	Mark
24	**If heart disease is chosen:** Stop smoking as chemicals in tobacco can damage the heart and blood vessels (1), causing narrowing of the arteries, which can lead to a heart attack (1). In the UK, patients can be referred to the NHS Stop Smoking Service which provides help and advice about the best way to quit (1). Education programmes and TV adverts raise awareness of the causes of heart disease (1). Laws in the UK have banned smoking in public places to reduce the chance of damage from secondary smoke (1). Regular exercise helps to control weight and reduce the chances of developing other conditions that put a strain on the heart, such as high blood pressure or high cholesterol (1). Eating a healthy diet can reduce the risk of heart disease, for example a diet rich in fruits, vegetables, whole grain and lean meats can prevent the build-up of fatty deposits around the heart (1). Medical advances in drugs and heart surgery can help to control heart disease (1). **If cancer is chosen:** Avoid smoking as cigarettes contain carcinogens like cyanide and ammonia, and can cause changes in the body leading to cancer of the lungs, mouth, throat, larynx, pancreas, bladder, cervix or kidneys (1). Some types of cancer are genetic, and regular check-ups and screening programmes can detect any changes to allow treatment to start earlier (1), so the death rate from cancer can be reduced (1). Treatment for cancer may include surgery to remove a tumour (1). People are encouraged to check themselves regularly for suspicious lumps and to see a doctor if they find any (1). Breast screening is carried out for women to identify any problems early (1). Chemotherapy and other drugs can be used to slow down the spread of cancer cells (1).	6

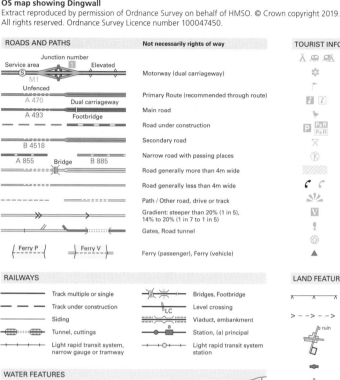

OS map showing Dingwall
Extract reproduced by permission of Ordnance Survey on behalf of HMSO. © Crown copyright 2019.
All rights reserved. Ordnance Survey Licence number 100047450.

1:50 000 Scale
Landranger Series

ROADS AND PATHS

Not necessarily rights of way

Motorway (dual carriageway)	
Primary Route (recommended through route)	
Main road	
Road under construction	
Secondary road	
Narrow road with passing places	
Road generally more than 4m wide	
Road generally less than 4m wide	
Path / Other road, drive or track	
Gradient: steeper than 20% (1 in 5), 14% to 20% (1 in 7 to 1 in 5)	
Gates, Road tunnel	
Ferry (passenger), Ferry (vehicle)	

Service area — Junction number — Elevated — M1 — Unfenced — A 470 — Dual carriageway — A 493 — Footbridge — B 4518 — A 855 — Bridge — B 885 — Ferry P — Ferry V

TOURIST INFORMATION

Camp site / caravan site	
Garden	
Golf course or links	
Information centre (all year / seasonal)	
Nature reserve	
Parking, Park and ride (all year / seasonal)	
Picnic site	
Recreation / leisure / sports centre	
Telephone, public / roadside assistance	
Viewpoint	
Visitor centre	
Walks / Trails	
World Heritage site or area	
Youth hostel	

RAILWAYS

Track multiple or single	Bridges, Footbridge
Track under construction	Level crossing
Siding	Viaduct, embankment
Tunnel, cuttings	Station, (a) principal
Light rapid transit system, narrow gauge or tramway	Light rapid transit system station

LAND FEATURES

Electricity transmission line (pylons shown at standard spacing)	
Pipe line (arrow indicates direction of flow)	
Buildings	
Important building (selected)	
Bus or coach station	
Current or former place of worship — with tower / with spire, minaret or dome	
Place of worship	
Glass structure	
Heliport	
Triangulation pillar	
Mast	
Wind pump, wind turbine	
Windmill with or without sails	
Graticule intersection at 5' intervals	
Cutting, embankment	
Landfill site or slag/spoil heap	
Coniferous wood	
Non-coniferous wood	
Mixed wood	
Orchard	
Park or ornamental ground	
Forestry Commission land	
National Trust (always open / limited access, observe local signs)	
National Trust for Scotland (always open / limited access, observe local signs)	

WATER FEATURES

Marsh or salting — Slopes — Cliff — Shingle — Towpath — Lock — Aqueduct — Canal — Ford — Flat rock — Lighthouse (in use) — Beacon — Lighthouse (disused) — Sand — Weir — Normal tidal limit — Dunes — Low water mark — Lake — Footbridge — Bridge — Mud — High water mark — Canal (dry)

HEIGHTS

1 metre = 3·2808 feet

Contours are at 10 metres vertical interval	
·144 Heights are to the nearest metre above mean sea level	

Where two heights are shown the first height is to the base of the triangulation pillar and the second (in brackets) to the highest natural point of the hill

ROCK FEATURES

Outcrop — Cliff — Scree

PUBLIC RIGHTS OF WAY

Footpath	
Bridleway	
Restricted byway	
Byway open to all traffic	

The symbols show the defined route so far as the scale of mapping will allow.

The representation on this map of any other road, track or path is no evidence of the existence of a right of way. Not shown on maps of Scotland

Danger Area — Firing and Test Ranges in the area. Danger! Observe warning notices.

OTHER PUBLIC ACCESS

• • • • Other route with public access (not normally shown in urban areas). Alignments are based on the best information available. These routes are not shown on maps of Scotland	
On-road cycle route	
Traffic-free cycle route	
4 National Cycle Network number	
8 Regional Cycle Network number	
◆◆ National Trail, European Long Distance Path, Long Distance Route, selected Recreational Routes	

BOUNDARIES

National	
District	
County, Unitary Authority, Metropolitan District or London Borough	
National Park	

ANTIQUITIES

+ Site of antiquity	
⚔ Battlefield (with date)	
☆ ···· Visible earthwork	
VILLA Roman	
Castle Non-Roman	

ABBREVIATIONS

Br	Bridge	MS	Milestone
Cemy	Cemetery	Mus	Museum
CG	Cattle grid	P	Post office
CH	Clubhouse	PC	Public convenience (in rural areas)
Fm	Farm	PH	Public house
Ho	House	Sch	School
MP	Milepost	TH	Town Hall, Guildhall or equivalent

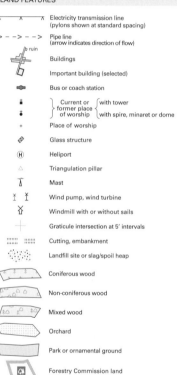

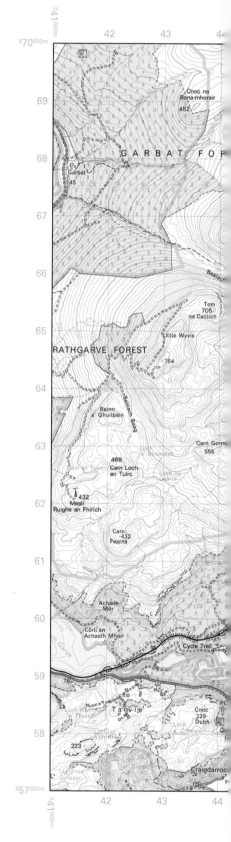

Extract No 1880/20

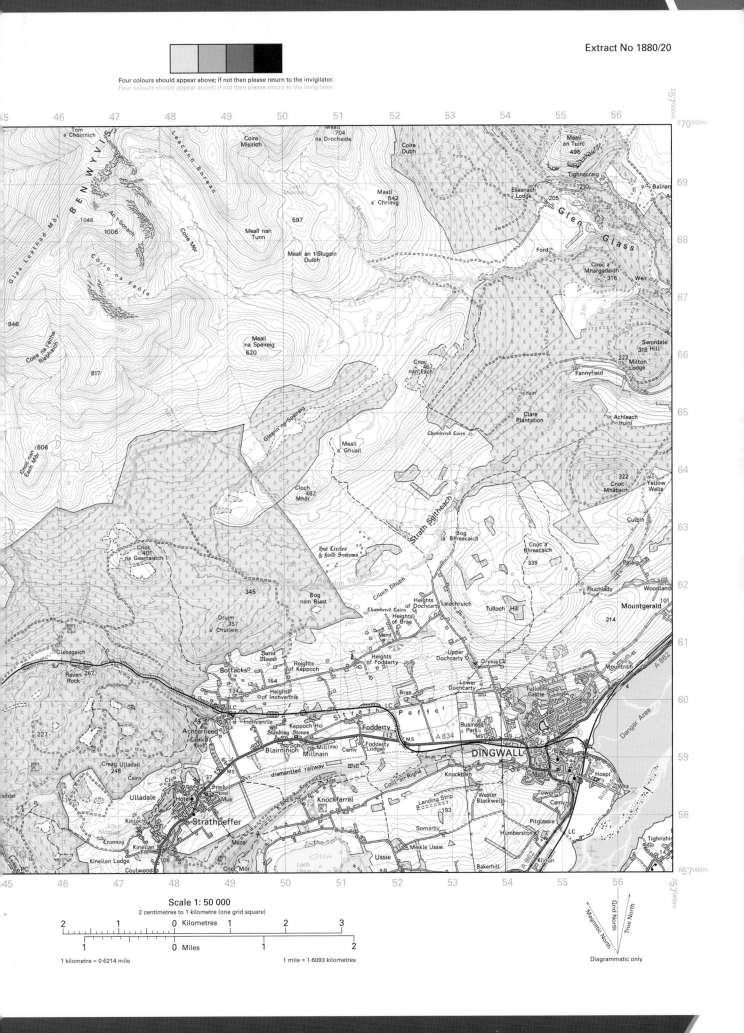

Four colours should appear above; if not then please return to the invigilator.

Scale 1: 50 000

2 centimetres to 1 kilometre (one grid square)

Kilometres

Miles

1 kilometre = 0·6214 mile

1 mile = 1·6093 kilometres

Grid North

True North

Magnetic North

Diagrammatic only

Ordnance Survey

1:50 000 Scale
Landranger Series

OS map showing Strathy
Extract produced by Ordnance Survey 2018. © Crown copyright 2019.

ROADS AND PATHS

Not necessarily rights of way

Junction number / Service area / Elevated / Unfenced	Motorway (dual carriageway)
A 470 / Dual carriageway	Primary Route (recommended through route)
A 493 / Footbridge	Main road
	Road under construction
B 4518	Secondary road
A 855 Bridge B 885	Narrow road with passing places
	Road generally more than 4m wide
	Road generally less than 4m wide
	Path / Other road, drive or track
	Gradient: steeper than 20% (1 in 5), 14% to 20% (1 in 7 to 1 in 5)
	Gates, Road tunnel
Ferry P / Ferry V	Ferry (passenger), Ferry (vehicle)

RAILWAYS

Track multiple or single		Bridges, footbridge	
Track under construction		Level crossing	
Siding		Viaduct, embankment	
Tunnel, cuttings		Station, (a) principal	
Light rapid transit system, narrow gauge or tramway		Light rapid transit system station	

WATER FEATURES

Marsh or salting
Slopes — Cliff
Towpath — Lock — Shingle
Aqueduct — Canal — Ford — Flat rock — Lighthouse (in use)
Weir — Beacon — Sand — Lighthouse (disused)
Lake — Footbridge — Bridge — Normal tidal limit — Dunes — Low water mark
Mud
High water mark
Canal (dry)

HEIGHTS

1 metre = 3·2808 feet

Contours are at 10 metres vertical interval

·144 Heights are to the nearest metre above mean sea level

Where two heights are shown the first height is to the base of the triangulation pillar and the second (in brackets) to the highest natural point of the hill

ROCK FEATURES

Outcrop
Cliff
Scree

PUBLIC RIGHTS OF WAY

············	Footpath
– – – – –	Bridleway
– · – · – ·	Restricted byway
–+–+–+–+	Byway open to all traffic

The symbols show the defined route so far as the scale of mapping will allow.

The representation on this map of any other road, track or path is no evidence of the existence of a right of way. Not shown on maps of Scotland

Danger Area — Firing and Test Ranges in the area. Danger! Observe warning notices.

OTHER PUBLIC ACCESS

· · · · Other route with public access (not normally shown in urban areas). Alignments are based on the best information available. These routes are not shown on maps of Scotland.

On-road cycle route
Traffic-free cycle route
4 National Cycle Network number
8 Regional Cycle Network number
National Trail, European Long Distance Path, Long Distance Route, selected Recreational Routes

BOUNDARIES

–+–+–	National
–+–·+–	District
–·–·–·–	County, Unitary Authority, Metropolitan District or London Borough
	National Park

ANTIQUITIES

+	Site of antiquity
⚔	Battlefield (with date)
☆ ····	Visible earthwork
VILLA	Roman
Castle	Non-Roman

TOURIST INFORMATION

⚔ 🏕 🚐	Camp site / caravan site
✿	Garden
⛳	Golf course or links
i i	Information centre (all year / seasonal)
⚘	Nature reserve
P P&R / P&R	Parking, Park and ride (all year / seasonal)
✕	Picnic site
Ⓡ	Recreation / leisure / sports centre
▨	Selected places of tourist interest
☎ ☎	Telephone, public / roadside assistance
☀	Viewpoint
V	Visitor centre
!	Walks / Trails
◎	World Heritage site or area
▲	Youth hostel

LAND FEATURES

⌐—⌐	Electricity transmission line (pylons shown at standard spacing)
> - -> - ->	Pipe line (arrow indicates direction of flow)
ruin	Buildings
	Important building (selected)
━	Bus or coach station
Current or former place of worship	with tower / with spire, minaret or dome
+	Place of worship
✿	Glass structure
Ⓗ	Heliport
△	Triangulation pillar
Ï	Mast
Ï Ï	Wind pump, wind turbine
Ⓧ	Windmill with or without sails
+	Graticule intersection at 5' intervals
⸬⸬	Cutting, embankment
∴∴∴	Landfill site or slag/spoil heap
	Coniferous wood
	Non-coniferous wood
	Mixed wood
	Orchard
	Park or ornamental ground
	Forestry Commission land
	National Trust (always open / limited access, observe local signs)
	National Trust for Scotland (always open / limited access, observe local signs)

ABBREVIATIONS

Br	Bridge	MS	Milestone
Cemy	Cemetery	Mus	Museum
CG	Cattle grid	P	Post office
CH	Clubhouse	PC	Public convenience (in rural areas)
Fm	Farm	PH	Public house
Ho	House	Sch	School
MP	Milepost	TH	Town Hall, Guildhall or equivalent

Magnetic North / Grid North / True North
Diagrammatic only

Scale 1: 50 000
2 centimetres to 1 kilometre (one grid square)

2 1 0 Kilometres 1 2 3

1 0 Miles 1 2

1 kilometre = 0·6214 mile   1 mile = 1·6093 kilometres

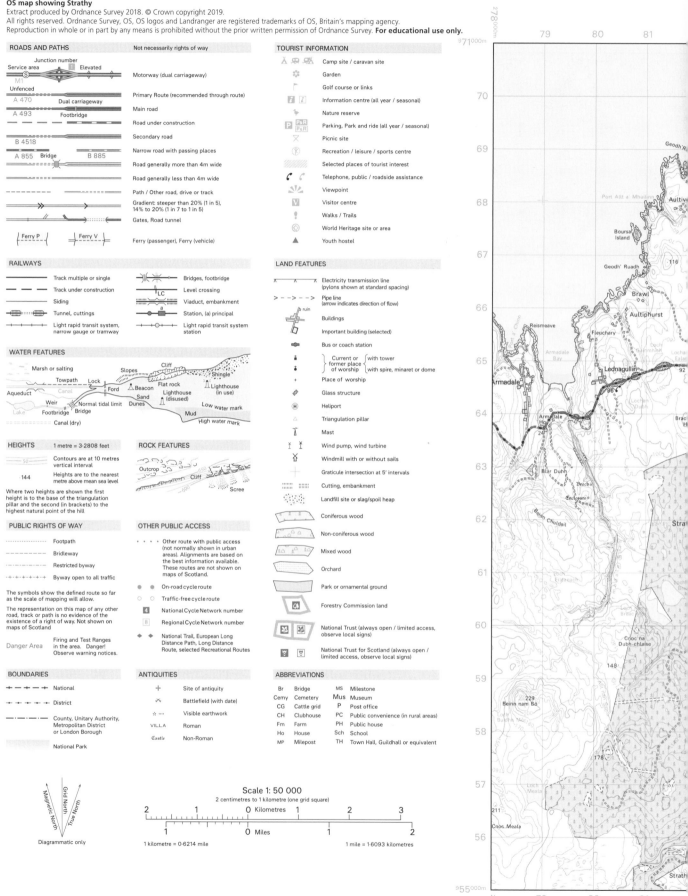

Extract No 2302/10

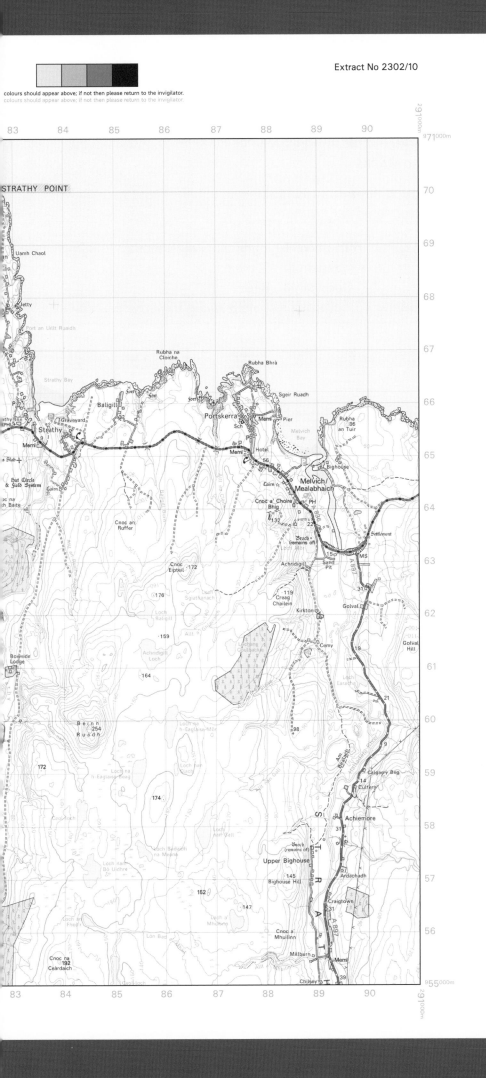

Duration: 2 hours, 20 minutes
Total marks: 80

SECTION 1 – PHYSICAL ENVIRONMENTS – 30 MARKS
Attempt EITHER question 1 OR question 2. ALSO attempt questions 3, 4, 5, 6 and 7.

SECTION 2 – HUMAN ENVIRONMENTS – 30 MARKS
Attempt questions 8, 9, 10, 11 and 12.

SECTION 3 – GLOBAL ISSUES – 20 MARKS
Attempt any TWO of the following:

Question 13 – Climate change
Question 14 – Natural regions
Question 15 – Environmental hazards

Question 16 – Trade and globalisation
Question 17 – Tourism
Question 18 – Health

Remember, you can use sketches, maps and diagrams (labelled appropriately) in your answer, where relevant.

Section 1: Physical environments

Total marks: 30
Attempt EITHER question 1 OR question 2 AND questions 3, 4, 5, 6 and 7.

MARKS

1 **Glaciated uplands/Coastal landscapes**
   Study the Ordnance Survey map extract of the Dingwall area.
   a   Match the glaciated upland features shown below with the correct grid reference.
       Features: truncated spur, corrie, U-shaped valley
       Choose from grid references:
       467677
       476683
       525594
       435663   3
   b   Explain the formation of headlands and bays.
       You may use a diagram(s) in your answer.   4

Now answer questions 3, 4, 5, 6 and 7
Do not answer this question if you have already answered question 1

2 **Rivers and their valleys**
   Study the Ordnance Survey map extract of the Dingwall area.
   a   Match the river features shown below with the correct grid reference.
       Features: V-shaped valley, meander, tributary
       Choose from grid references:
       528595
       442591
       447585
       473657   3
   b   Explain the formation of a waterfall.
       You may use a diagram(s) in your answer.   4

Now answer questions 3, 4, 5, 6 and 7

3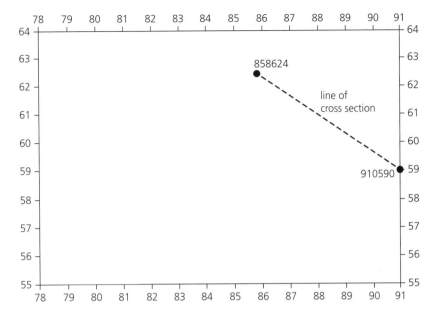

Diagram Q3A: Cross section GR 858624 to GR 910590

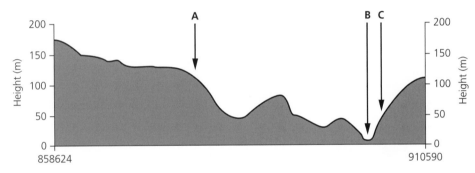

Diagram Q3B: Cross section

Study the Ordnance Survey map extract of the Strathy area and Diagrams Q3A and Q3B.

Match the letters A–C with the correct features.

Choose from the features below.

3

Halladale River; track; forestry; electricity transmission lines

4

Diagram Q4: Land uses in the map extract area

Look at Diagram Q4.

Choose one land use from Diagram Q4. Using map evidence, explain the advantages the area of the map extract has for your chosen land use.

5

5

Landscape Types
Glaciated uplands
Upland limestone
Coastal landscapes
Rivers and valleys

Diagram Q5: Selected land use conflicts

Study Diagram Q5.

Choose one landscape type from Diagram Q5 and, referring to an area you have studied, explain strategies which can be used to reduce land use conflicts in your chosen area.

6

6

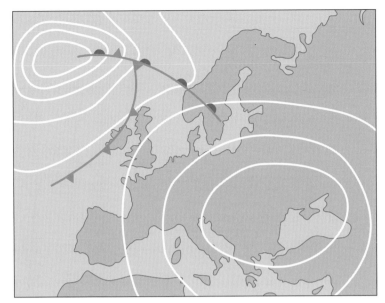

Diagram Q6A: Synoptic chart, 25 July 2016

High pressure looks set to continue in the Mediterranean for the rest of the month. It should be dry with mainly clear skies and long spells of sunshine. Temperatures are expected to be around 27 °C, the average for this time of the year. In the UK, changeable conditions will persist. Temperatures should average around 14 °C. Northern and western parts of the UK could see spells of rain and wind at times.

Diagram Q6B: Weather forecast for the Mediterranean and the UK

Study Diagrams Q6A and Q6B.

Explain the forecasts for the Mediterranean area and the UK. You should refer to the synoptic chart in your answer.

5

7

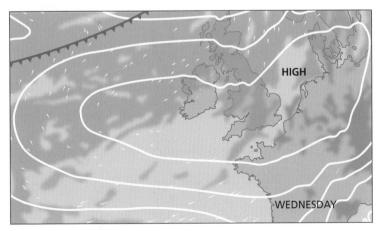

Diagram Q7: Anticyclone over the UK

Study Diagram Q7.

Anticyclones bring different weather conditions throughout the year. Describe the advantages and disadvantages of an anticyclone in summer.

4

Now go to Section 2

OS map showing Preston

Extract reproduced by permission of Ordnance Survey on behalf of HMSO. © Crown copyright 2019.
All rights reserved. Ordnance Survey Licence number 100047450.

1:50 000 Scale
Landranger Series

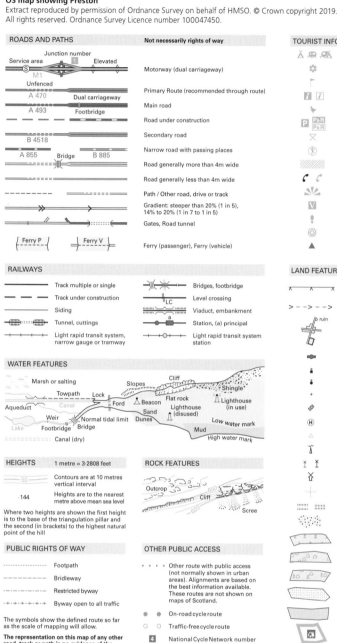

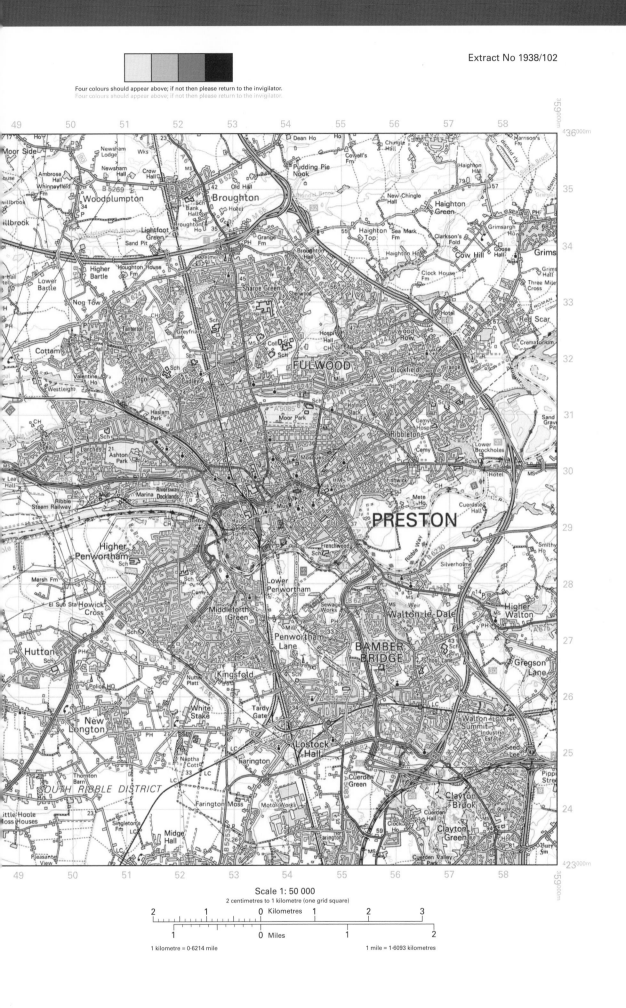

Four colours should appear above; if not then please return to the invigilator.

Scale 1: 50 000

2 centimetres to 1 kilometre (one grid square)

1 kilometre = 0·6214 mile

1 mile = 1·6093 kilometres

Section 2: Human environments

Total marks: 30

Attempt questions 8, 9, 10, 11 and 12.

8

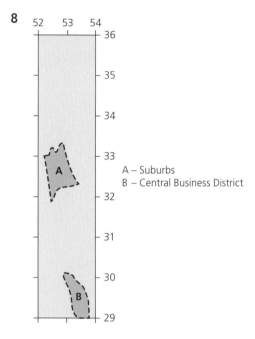

A – Suburbs
B – Central Business District

Diagram Q8: Selected land use zones in Preston

Study Diagram Q8 and the Ordnance Survey map extract of the Preston area.

Mr Bailey's S4 class has completed an urban land use survey for their National 5 assignment. They identified area A as the suburbs and area B as the CBD of Preston. Using map evidence, describe in detail the reasons for their decisions.

5

9 Study the Ordnance Survey map extract of the Preston area.

Measure the three distances (A, B and C) between the places shown in the table.

Match your answers for A, B and C with the distances given below.

A	The school at 4926 to Sea Mark Farm at 5534
B	The public house (PH) at 5727 to the golf course at 5432
C	The works at 5135 to the college at 5332

Choose from: 6.5 km   4.2 km   3.5 km   10 km

3

10 Study the Ordnance Survey map extract of the Preston area.

An industrial estate is found at 5725. Using map evidence, give reasons why features like industrial estates are found on the rural/urban fringe.

6

MARKS

11

Indicators	UK	Chad
GNP per capita	$37,000	$826
Literacy rate	99%	47%
People per doctor	400	20,000
Life expectancy	81	51
% employed in agriculture	1%	78%

Diagram Q11: Selected indicators of development for the UK and Chad

Study Diagram Q11.

a Describe, in detail, the differences in development between Chad and the United Kingdom.

4

b Choose two indicators from Diagram Q11. For each indicator, give reasons for the differences between a developed country like the UK and a developing country like Chad.

6

12

Diagram Q12: Asian farmer studying farm data

Study Diagram Q12.
Explain the advantages and disadvantages which modern developments in agriculture have brought to developing countries.

6

Now go to Section 3

Section 3: Global issues

Total marks: 20

Attempt any TWO questions.

Question 13 – Climate change

Question 14 – Natural regions

Question 15 – Environmental hazards

Question 16 – Trade and globalisation

Question 17 – Tourism

Question 18 – Health

MARKS

13 Climate change

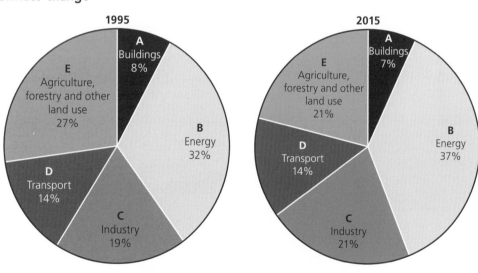

Diagram Q13A: Greenhouse gas emissions

a   Study Diagram Q13A.

Describe, in detail, the changes in greenhouse gas emissions between 1995 and 2015.

4

Sea level rise: according to the UK Met Office, sea levels around the UK have risen about 10 centimetres since 1900.

Changes in rainfall: rainfall in the UK during summer is decreasing, while in winter it is increasing.

UK Met Office

Diagram Q13B: Some effects of climate change

b   Look at Diagram Q13B.

Describe, in detail, ways in which people try to manage climate change.

6

14 Natural regions

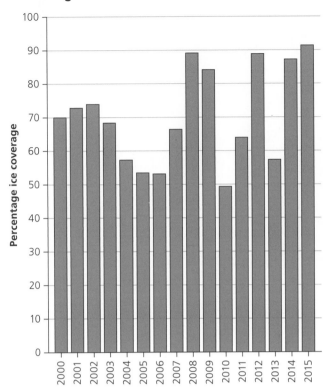

Diagram Q14A: Percentage ice cover 2000–2015

a Study Diagram Q14A.

Describe, in detail, the changes in the percentage of ice cover between 2000 and 2015.

4

> Natural resources: any natural substance that living things can use
>
> Examples: air, water, sunlight, soil, minerals, plants, animals, forests, fossil fuels

Diagram Q14B: Natural resources

b Look at Diagram Q14B.

For either the rainforest or the tundra, explain ways in which recent human activities affect the people and the environment of your chosen area.

6

15 Environmental hazards

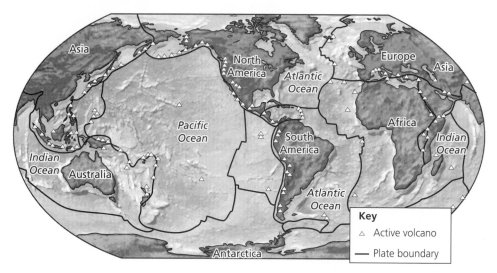

Diagram Q15: Active volcanoes

Study Diagram Q15.

a Describe, in detail, the distribution of the Earth's active volcanoes.

4

b Referring to a named hurricane, earthquake or volcano you have studied, explain strategies used to reduce its effects.

6

16 Trade and globalisation

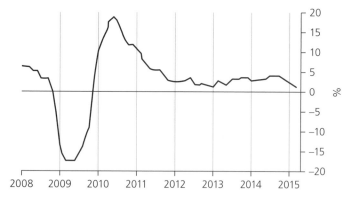

Diagram Q16A: Changing percentage volume of world trade

a Study Diagram Q16A.

Describe, in detail, the changes in the percentage volume of world trade between 2008 and 2015.

4

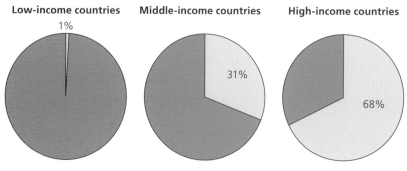

Diagram Q16B: Share of world trade/GDP

b Look at Diagram Q16B.

Explain the causes of inequalities in world trade.

6

17 Tourism

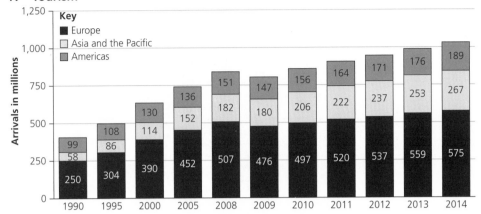

Diagram Q17: Selected international tourist arrivals 1990–2014

Study Diagram Q17.

a Describe, in detail, the changes in international tourist arrivals 1990–2014.

4

b Explain the impact of mass tourism on the people and environment.
In your answer, you should refer to areas you have studied.

6

18 Health

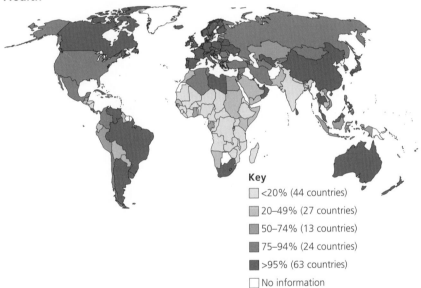

Diagram Q18A: Access to health care

a Study Diagram Q18A.

Describe, in detail, the differences in access to health care across the world.

4

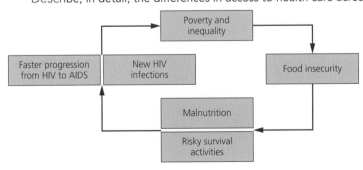

Diagram Q18B: Impact of HIV/AIDS

b Look at Diagram Q18B.

Explain methods used to control the spread of HIV/AIDS.

6

[End of Practice Paper 1]

OS map showing Swansea

Extract reproduced by permission of Ordnance
Survey on behalf of HMSO. © Crown copyright 2019.
All rights reserved. Ordnance Survey Licence
number 100047450.
For a detailed key, please refer to page 66.
Scale 1:50 000

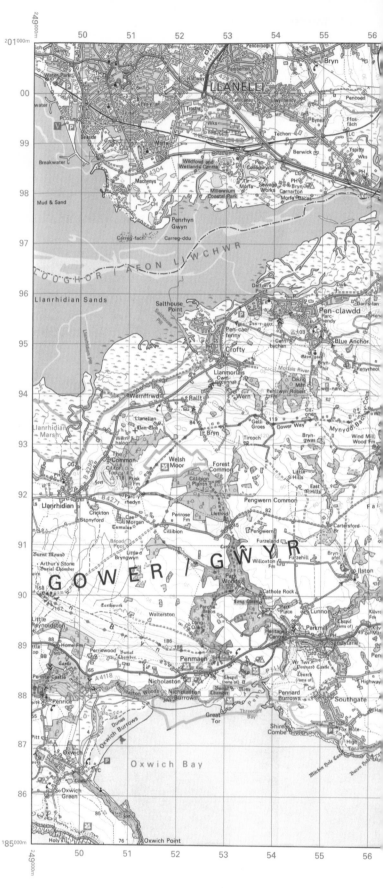

Diagrammatic only

Scale 1: 50 000

2 centimetres to 1 kilometre (one grid square)

2   1   0   Kilometres   1   2   3

1   0   Miles   1   2

1 kilometre = 0·6214 mile   1 mile = 1·6093 kilometres

Ordnance Survey®

1:50 000 Scale
Landranger Series

OS map showing East Kilbride

Extract reproduced by permission of Ordnance Survey on behalf of HMSO. © Crown copyright 2019.
All rights reserved. Ordnance Survey Licence number 100047450.

ROADS AND PATHS

Not necessarily rights of way

Junction number

Service area / Elevated
Motorway (dual carriageway)
M1

Unfenced
A 470 Dual carriageway
Primary Route (recommended through route)

A 493 Footbridge
Main road

Road under construction

B 4518
Secondary road

A 855 Bridge B 885
Narrow road with passing places

Road generally more than 4m wide

Road generally less than 4m wide

Path / Other road, drive or track

Gradient: steeper than 20% (1 in 5), 14% to 20% (1 in 7 to 1 in 5)

Gates, Road tunnel

Ferry P / Ferry V
Ferry (passenger), Ferry (vehicle)

RAILWAYS

Track multiple or single
Bridges, footbridge

Track under construction
LC Level crossing

Siding
Viaduct, embankment

Tunnel, cuttings
Station, (a) principal

Light rapid transit system, narrow gauge or tramway
Light rapid transit system station

WATER FEATURES

Marsh or salting
Cliff
Slopes
Shingle

Towpath Lock
Flat rock
Beacon
Lighthouse (in use)

Aqueduct Canal
Ford
Sand
Lighthouse (disused)

Weir
Normal tidal limit
Low water mark
Lake Footbridge Bridge Dunes

Mud

Canal (dry)
High water mark

HEIGHTS

1 metre = 3·2808 feet

50 — Contours are at 10 metres vertical interval

·144 Heights are to the nearest metre above mean sea level

Where two heights are shown the first height is to the base of the triangulation pillar and the second (in brackets) to the highest natural point of the hill

ROCK FEATURES

Outcrop

Cliff

Scree

PUBLIC RIGHTS OF WAY

· · · · · · · Footpath

– – – – – – Bridleway

-·-·-·-·- Restricted byway

-+-+-+-+- Byway open to all traffic

The symbols show the defined route so far as the scale of mapping will allow.

The representation on this map of any other road, track or path is no evidence of the existence of a right of way. Not shown on maps of Scotland

Danger Area
Firing and Test Ranges in the area. Danger! Observe warning notices.

OTHER PUBLIC ACCESS

· · · · Other route with public access (not normally shown in urban areas). Alignments are based on the best information available. These routes are not shown on maps of Scotland.

● ○ On-road cycle route

● ○ Traffic-free cycle route

4 National Cycle Network number

8 Regional Cycle Network number

◆ ◆ National Trail, European Long Distance Path, Long Distance Route, selected Recreational Routes

BOUNDARIES

+ – + – + National

+ · + · + · + District

– · – · – · – County, Unitary Authority, Metropolitan District or London Borough

National Park

ANTIQUITIES

+ Site of antiquity

⚔ Battlefield (with date)

☆ ···· Visible earthwork

VILLA Roman

Castle Non-Roman

TOURIST INFORMATION

⚑ 🚐 🚻 Camp site / caravan site

❀ Garden

⛳ Golf course or links

i Information centre (all year / seasonal)

P P&R Parking, Park and ride (all year / seasonal)

✕ Picnic site

Recreation / leisure / sports centre

Selected places of tourist interest

☎ Telephone, public / roadside assistance

Viewpoint

V Visitor centre

! Walks / Trails

◎ World Heritage site or area

▲ Youth hostel

LAND FEATURES

Electricity transmission line (pylons shown at standard spacing)

> - - > - - Pipe line (arrow indicates direction of flow)

ruin Buildings

Important building (selected)

Bus or coach station

Current or former place of worship { with tower / with spire, minaret or dome

+ Place of worship

Glass structure

H Heliport

△ Triangulation pillar

Mast

Wind pump, wind turbine

Windmill with or without sails

Graticule intersection at 5' intervals

Cutting, embankment

Landfill site or slag/spoil heap

Coniferous wood

Non-coniferous wood

Mixed wood

Orchard

Park or ornamental ground

Forestry Commission land

National Trust (always open / limited access, observe local signs)

National Trust for Scotland (always open / limited access, observe local signs)

ABBREVIATIONS

Br	Bridge	MS	Milestone
Cemy	Cemetery	Mus	Museum
CG	Cattle grid	P	Post office
CH	Clubhouse	PC	Public convenience (in rural areas)
Fm	Farm	PH	Public house
Ho	House	Sch	School
MP	Milepost	TH	Town Hall, Guildhall or equivalent

Magnetic North / Grid North / True North

Diagrammatic only

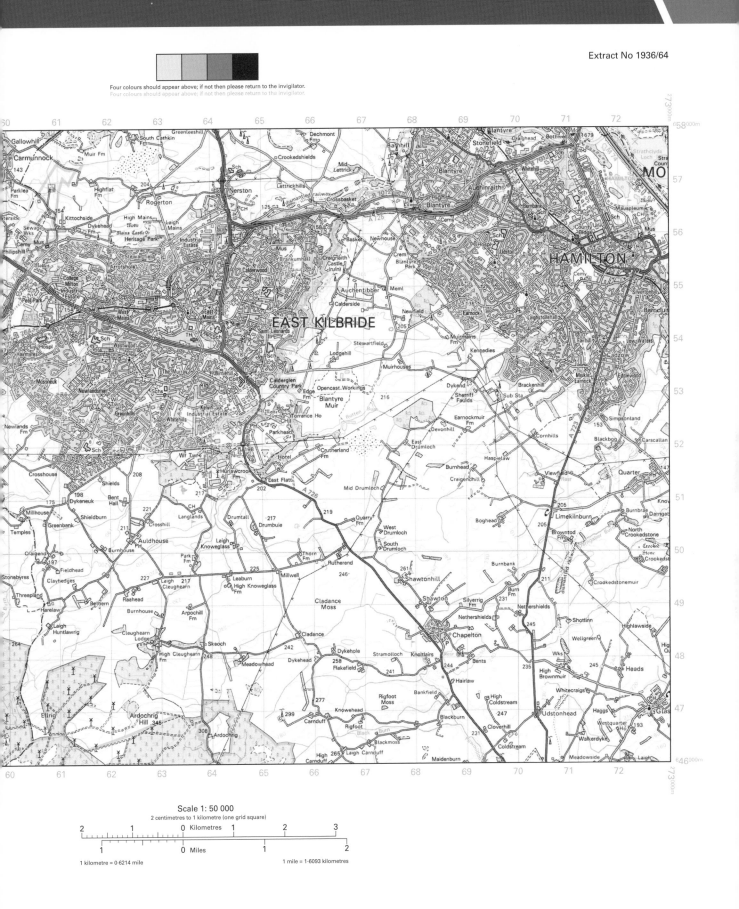

Scale 1: 50 000

2 centimetres to 1 kilometre (one grid square)

1 kilometre = 0·6214 mile

1 mile = 1·6093 kilometres

Duration: 2 hours, 20 minutes

Total marks: 80

SECTION 1 – PHYSICAL ENVIRONMENTS – 30 MARKS

Attempt EITHER question 1 OR question 2. ALSO attempt questions 3, 4, 5 and 6.

SECTION 2 – HUMAN ENVIRONMENTS – 30 MARKS

Attempt questions 7, 8, 9, 10 and 11.

SECTION 3 – GLOBAL ISSUES – 20 MARKS

Attempt any TWO of the following:

Question 12 – Climate change

Question 13 – Natural regions

Question 14 – Environmental hazards

Question 15 – Trade and globalisation

Question 16 – Tourism

Question 17 – Health

Remember, you can use sketches, maps and diagrams (labelled appropriately) in your answer, where relevant.

Section 1: Physical environments

Total marks: 30

Attempt EITHER question 1 OR question 2 AND questions 3, 4, 5 and 6.

MARKS

1 Coastal landscapes/Glaciated landscapes

Study the Ordnance Survey map extract of the Swansea area.

a Match the coastal features shown below with the correct grid reference.

Features: headland, stack, bay

Choose from grid references:

612869   535877   570863   555869

3

b Explain the formation of a corrie.

You may use a diagram or diagrams in your answer.

4

Now answer questions 3, 4, 5 and 6

Do not answer this question if you have already answered question 1

2 Rivers and their valleys

Study the Ordnance Survey map extract of the East Kilbride area.

a Match the river features shown below with the correct grid reference.

Features: V-shaped valley, meander, waterfall

Choose from grid references:

591515   684505   652516   575535

3

b Explain the formation of a V-shaped valley.

You may use a diagram or diagrams in your answer.

4

3 Study the Ordnance Survey map extract of the Swansea area.

Using map evidence, explain ways in which the physical landscape has affected land use on the map extract.

6

4

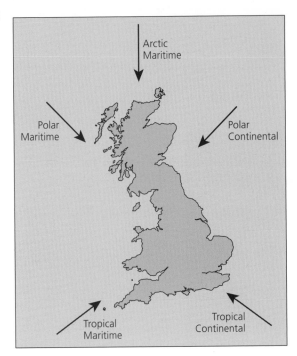

Diagram Q4: Air masses affecting the UK

Study Diagram Q4.

Describe, in detail, the advantages and disadvantages a polar continental air mass brings to the UK in winter.

4

5

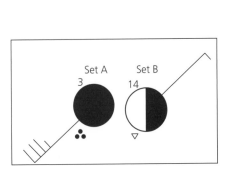

Diagram Q5A: Two sets of weather data for Birmingham

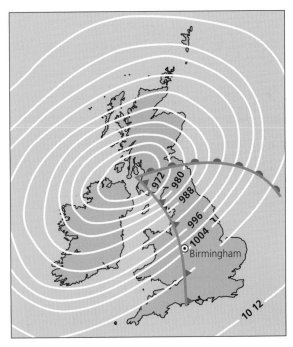

Diagram Q5B: Synoptic chart for the UK, 25 December 2018

a Study Diagram Q5A.
Describe the differences in weather conditions between set A and set B.

3

b Study Diagrams Q5A and Q5B.
Which set of weather data, A or B, is accurate for Birmingham?
Use the synoptic chart to give reasons for your choice.

5

6

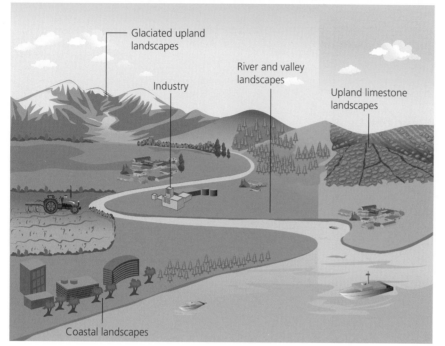

Glaciated upland
landscapes

Industry

River and valley
landscapes

Upland limestone
landscapes

Coastal landscapes

Land uses

• Farming • Forestry • Recreation • Water storage • Renewable
                          and tourism   and supply   energy

Diagram Q6: Landscape types and land uses in the UK

Look at Diagram Q6.

Choose one landscape type you have studied from Diagram Q6.

Select two land uses from Diagram Q6 and explain why these land uses are in
conflict with each other.

5

Now go to Section 2

Section 2: Human environments

Total marks: 30
Attempt questions 7, 8, 9, 10 and 11.

MARKS

7 Study the Ordnance Survey map extract of the Hamilton/East Kilbride area.

   a Give map evidence to show that the CBD of Hamilton is found in grid
      square 7255.

      3

   b East Kilbride has industrial estates found on the edge of the town,
      for example, Kelvin Industrial Estate at 640525.
      Using map evidence, explain why these developments are found on the
      edge of town.

      5

8 Study the Ordnance Survey map extract of the Hamilton/East Kilbride area.

   It has been proposed to build new housing at Brackenhill in grid square 7053.

   Using map evidence, explain why this area is suitable for new housing.

   5

9

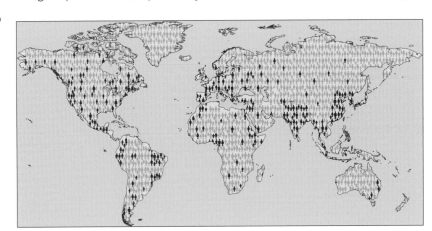

Diagram Q9: World population density map

Look at Diagram Q9.

Give reasons why population is not spread evenly across the world. You should
refer to both human and physical factors in your answer.

6

10

Diagram Q10: Shanty town in Kolkata, India

Look at Diagram Q10.

For a named developing world city you have studied, describe methods used by
city authorities to improve living conditions in shanty towns.

5

11

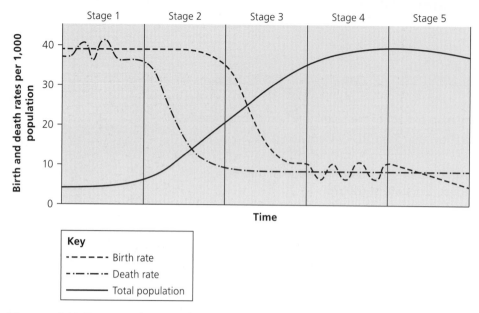

Diagram Q11: Demographic Transition Model

Look at Diagram Q11.

Explain, in detail, the changes in birth and death rates at stages 3 and 4 of the Demographic Transition Model.

6

Now go to Section 3

Section 3: Global issues

Total marks: 20

Attempt any TWO questions.

Question 12 – Climate change

Question 13 – Natural regions

Question 14 – Environmental hazards

Question 15 – Trade and globalisation

Question 16 – Tourism

Question 17 – Health

12 Climate change

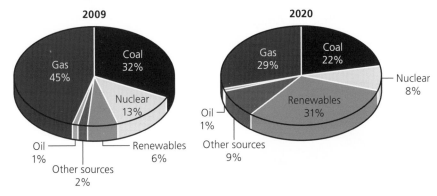

Diagram Q12A: UK energy generation

a Study Diagram Q12A.

Describe, in detail, the differences in energy generation between 2009 and 2020.

4

Diagram Q12B: Paris Climate Change Summit 2015

b Look at Diagram Q12B.

Explain the local and global effects of climate change on people and the environment. You should refer to named examples you have studied in your answer.

6

MARKS

13 Natural regions

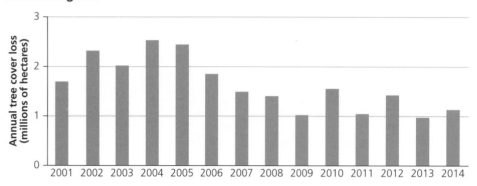

Diagram Q13A: Tree cover loss in the Brazilian Amazon 2001–2014

a Study Diagram Q13A.

Describe, in detail, the tree cover loss in the Brazilian Amazon, 2001–2014.

4

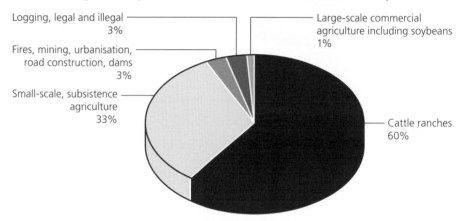

Diagram Q13B: Land use in the rainforest

b Look at Diagram Q13B.

Choose two land uses from Diagram Q13B.
Explain how your chosen land uses can lead to destruction of the rainforest.

6

14 Environmental hazards

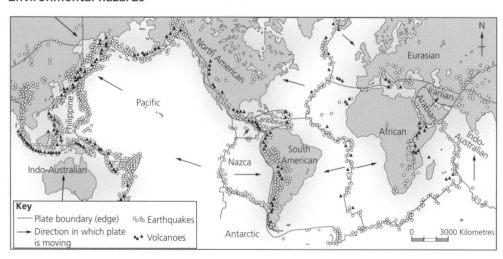

Diagram Q14A: Distribution of earthquakes and volcanoes

a Study Diagram Q14A.

Describe, in detail, the distribution of earthquakes.

4

Diagram Q14B: Selected natural disasters

b Look at Diagram Q14B.

For a named environmental hazard you have studied, explain methods used to predict and plan for its occurrence.

6

15 Trade and globalisation

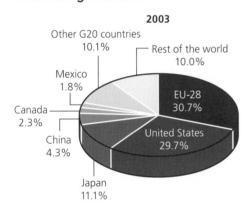 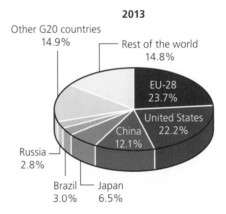

Diagram Q15A: Share of world GDP

a Study Diagram Q15A.

Describe, in detail, the changes in the share of world global trade between 2003 and 2013.

4

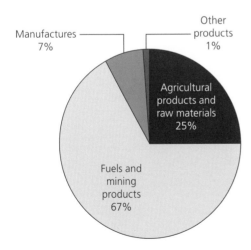

Diagram Q15B: Exports of a developing country

b Look at Diagram Q15B.

Many developing countries rely on one product to export. Explain the effects that changing demand for the product will have on the country.

6

MARKS

16 Tourism

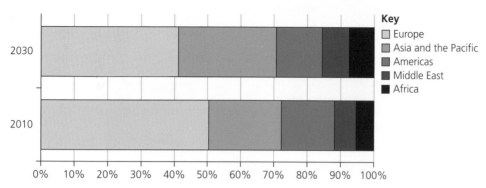

Diagram Q16A: International tourist arrivals by destination 2010–2030 (projected)

a Study Diagram Q16A.

Describe, in detail, the projected changes in international tourist arrivals 2010–2030.

4

Diagram Q16B: Ecotourism

b Look at Diagram Q16B.

Explain the advantages that ecotourism brings to the people and environment of a developing country.
You should refer to an area you have studied in your answer.

6

17 Health

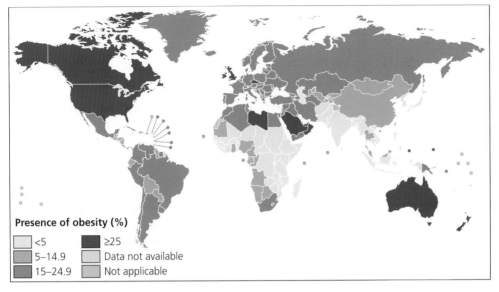

Diagram Q17A: Presence of obesity (%) in men over the age of 18 (2014)

a Study Diagram Q17A.

Describe, in detail, the world distribution of obesity in men over the age of 18.

4

- Every seven minutes someone in the UK will have a heart attack

- Globally smoking causes 71% of lung cancers

- In the UK 37% of men and 28% of women regularly exceed the government's recommendations for alcohol

Diagram Q17B: Selected health facts 2016

b Look at Diagram Q17B.

For **either** heart disease, cancer **or** asthma, explain the main causes of your chosen disease.

6

[End of Practice Paper 2]

ANSWERS TO PRACTICE PAPERS

Practice Paper 1

Section 1: Physical environments

Question	Expected answer	Mark	Commentary with hints and tips
1a	Truncated spur: 476683 Corrie: 467677 U-shaped valley: 525594	3	First match the features you are sure are correct. You can then match any remaining feature to its reference. Do not leave a feature without a reference. Even if you do not know the correct answer, make a guess at the remaining references as you could be lucky and match them correctly!
1b	Headlands and bays are found in areas where there are bands of alternating hard and soft rock (1) which meet the coast at right angles (1). The softer rock, for example clay, erodes more quickly, forming bays (1), while the harder rock, for example chalk, erodes more slowly, forming headlands (1). When formed, the bays then become sheltered by the headlands as they erode less (1). Once formed, the headland is then left more at risk from erosion as the waves' energy is concentrated here (1).	4	The more detail you put into an answer, the more marks you will gain. If you simply refer to processes like erosion or deposition, you will gain only 1 mark. However, you will gain additional marks if you explain the processes. You can gain a mark from drawing a series of diagrams which shows how the feature is formed at different stages. A diagram with labels which explains the formation can gain full marks.
2a	V-shaped valley: 473657 Meander: 447585 Tributary: 528595	3	Match the features you are sure are correct. You can then match the remaining feature to its reference. Do not leave a feature without a reference. Even if you do not know the correct answer, make a guess at the remaining references as you could be lucky and match them correctly!
2b	Waterfalls are found where hard rock like limestone overlies softer rock like mudstone (1). The water is powerful and erodes the softer rock by hydraulic action (1). This is the force of the water hitting the rock (1). Over time a plunge pool forms (1). The softer rock is worn away and the hard rock is undercut (1) and an overhang of hard rock is left suspended above the plunge pool (1). This collapses as there is nothing to support it and the rock falls into the plunge pool (1). Rock fragments swirling around deepen the plunge pool (1). This process is repeated over a long period of time and the waterfall retreats upstream forming a steep-sided gorge (1).	4	The more detail you put into an answer, the more marks you will gain. If you simply refer to river processes like hydraulic action, attrition, corrosion and corrasion, you will gain only 1 mark. However, you will gain additional marks if you explain the processes. You can gain a mark for drawing a series of diagrams which shows how the feature is formed at different stages. A diagram with labels which explains the formation can gain full marks.

Question	Expected answer	Mark	Commentary with hints and tips
3	A – Forestry B – Halladale River C – Electricity transmission lines	3	Even if you are not sure of the answer, do not leave blanks. You might be lucky and guess the correct answer!
4	**If recreation and tourism is chosen:** There is a variety of scenery, e.g. glaciated mountains, rivers and coasts attracting a range of visitors, from sightseers to photographers (1). There are mountains which can be used for climbing and walking (1). Water activities like sailing or windsurfing are possible in the surrounding rivers and lochs, for example Loch Garve (1) at 412592 (1). There are forested areas which can be used for walking, birdwatching and picnicking, for example at 481611 (1). Flat land near the coast is suitable for tourist accommodation in the form of caravan and campsites (1). **If forestry is chosen:** Large parts of the map area are very steep and would be unsuitable for most other land uses (1). Many of the slopes are too steep to use machinery (1). Much of the land is high and too cold for crops to grow (1). Soils might be acidic and there is likely to be plenty of rainfall, but coniferous trees can grow in these conditions (1), and there is access via the A834 to transport the logs to market (1).	5	Make sure you read the question. This question is asking you to explain why the area in the map extract is suitable for your chosen land use. This means you must give reasons in your answer. Your answer must refer to map evidence. Giving an appropriate grid reference (preferably a six-figure grid reference) will gain you a mark. Do not list the type of activities that you identify on the map – this is simple description, for example: 'The area can be used to ski, climb, sail, etc.' What you should say is: 'There are mountains in the area which have steep slopes which are good for skiing.' Name the feature on the map, then give the reason why it is good for your chosen land use. Examples are given for four different land uses. You would only need to answer on one land use.

Question	Expected answer	Mark	Commentary with hints and tips
5	**Glaciated upland areas** **If the Lake District is chosen:** Areas like the Lake District and Loch Lomond are designated as National Parks so the landscape is protected by law (1). To prevent traffic congestion in the small villages and to prevent inconsiderate parking, the number of car parks have been increased (1). In some areas, park-and-ride schemes have been created to reduce the amount of traffic on the small country roads as well as in the villages (1). Bodies such as the National Parks Authority try to educate the public through the use of leaflets, presentations and well-informed park rangers to talk to the visitors (2). Information boards at important sites and car parks give specific details about a site and advice on access (2). Construction of ladder stiles over walls and step stiles through fences where rights of way cross field boundaries prevents these getting destroyed by walkers, etc. (2). Visitors are encouraged by signposts to keep to the public footpaths to reduce footpath erosion (1). Notices are put up during lambing time to ask visitors to be especially considerate of farmers' needs, e.g. keep dogs on a lead (2). Building in these areas is controlled and permission has to be given for any new structures (1). **Coastal landscapes** **If the Dorset coast is chosen:** The Dorset coast has been designated a World Heritage Site, and there are strict planning controls that allow local authorities to protect the coast from over-development (1). Recreational activities like boating, yachting, fishing, etc. take place in Poole Harbour so zoning of areas ensures that different activities are kept apart (1). Speed limits have also been put in place reducing the danger to other users as well as reducing the erosional effects on the shoreline (2). Additional parking and alternative types of transport like train lines and new bus routes have been introduced to reduce traffic congestion and pollution (1). Nature reserves have been created to protect local wildlife and to try to reduce the impact of tourists using the beaches (1). Fines have been introduced to deter people from dropping litter (1). Rangers are employed to prevent problems and to educate visitors (1).	6	Make sure you refer to a specific area you have studied. Sometimes marks can be lost if you give a general answer. Marks will not be given for describing the land use conflicts – you must give strategies to solve the conflicts. Remember, if the question is worth 6 marks, you need to make six points to get the marks. Examples are given for coastal landscapes and glaciated upland landscapes. You only need to answer on one landscape.

Question	Expected answer	Mark	Commentary with hints and tips
6	The Mediterranean has an area of high pressure over it and high-pressure systems bring settled weather lasting for a period of time (1). Conditions are clear as high pressure in summer brings limited cloud cover (1). There are no fronts over the area so there is no rainfall (1). The isobars are far apart so there are gentle winds (1). The temperature is high, which is typical of high pressure in this area in the summer (1). The UK is experiencing a depression which brings changeable weather (1). Depressions bring clouds, causing overcast conditions (1). There is a front close to the NW of the UK which will bring rain (1). Winds will be strong as the isobars are close together (1).	5	Before you start to answer a weather question with a synoptic chart, you must always check the date of the chart. The weather will be different depending on the time of year, especially for an anticyclone. Do not describe the weather or list the weather – this will gain you very few marks. You need to interpret the chart to give reasons for the weather being experienced.
7	**Advantages:** Warm, dry and sunny weather improves people's mood (1). People can participate in more outdoor activities such as BBQs (1). Outdoor sports can take place, e.g. tennis matches, without being rained off (1). School sports days can safely go ahead due to dry conditions (1). Rising sales of summer goods such as sunscreen and ice lollies increase shops' profits (1). **Disadvantages:** Hosepipe bans may be enforced due to a lack of water (1). Drought conditions reduce the yield of farmers' crops (1). People suffer from sunburn and dehydration (1). More people are admitted to hospital with heatstroke (1) putting a strain on resources (1). Forest fires break out (1). Thunderstorms are also a disadvantage of anticyclones (1).	4	Remember to give both advantages and disadvantages in your answer.

Section 2: Human environments

Question	Expected answer	Mark	Commentary with hints and tips
8	**Area A: The suburbs** The suburbs are located closer to the edge of Preston so have been built more recently (1). There is more open space than in the CBD, which is in the centre of town (1). The patterns of the streets are curvilinear with cul-de-sacs (1), as shown at grid reference 524328 (1). Amenities like a hospital, leisure centre and several schools have been provided for the residents (1). **Area B: The central business district** This is the CBD as it is in the centre of the town (1). The main transport routes meet here (1). It has a main railway station at 536290 (1). There is a tourist information centre (1) and a museum (1). There are many churches, indicating that it is the oldest part of town (1).	5	For full marks you must refer to both areas. You must use map evidence in your answer. Refer to specific examples from the map. You may gain a mark from giving an appropriate grid reference.
9	A – 10 km B – 6.5 km C – 4.2 km	3	Remember to look at the scale of the map and to convert your measurement from centimetres to kilometres.

Question	Expected answer	Mark	Commentary with hints and tips
10	The land is flat so it is easier to build on (1). The area is away from the busy CBD so it is less congested, allowing traffic to flow in and out of the area more quickly (1). There is some empty land in the square so there is room for expansion in the future (1). The area is accessible via roads like the M61, A6 and A49 (1). There is also a railway line running through the square with a station close by (1). There is housing at Walton Summit providing a workforce for the industrial estate (1) as well as customers (1).	6	These answers are map evidence. You should not necessarily just make six points (as there are 6 marks) as some might be wrong. By making more than six points, the extra points are a backup to ensure you get maximum marks.
11a	The UK has a far greater GNP by $36,174 (1). The UK has a literacy rate of 99% which is 52% higher than Chad's (1). Only 22% of the population of Chad are employed outside agriculture whereas in the UK this figure is 99% (1). People in Chad are expected to live for 30 years fewer than those in the UK (1). There are far more people per doctor in Chad than there are in the UK (1) – by 19,600 (1).	4	In this question, you must use figures to gain full marks. General statements like higher or lower/ increasing or decreasing might only gain you 2 marks. Try to process the information. Instead of saying the UK has a higher life expectancy at 81 than Chad at only 51, you could say: 'In the UK people are expected to live until they are 81 which is 30 years more than in Chad.'
11b	**If life expectancy is chosen:** Countries with a high life expectancy like the UK have the money to invest in health care (1). They have hospitals, modern technology and drugs to keep people healthier (1). Jobs are less strenuous and less dangerous, which improves life expectancy (1). Money is invested in the elderly, resulting in better life expectancy (1). **If percentage employed in agriculture is chosen:** In countries like the UK, a low percentage of people are employed in agriculture as there is money available to invest in industry (1) so more people are employed in industry. This means people have a higher standard of living (1) due to higher wages (1). Countries with a low percentage of people employed in agriculture can afford to import food from other countries rather than grow it all themselves (1).	6	You are asked to choose two indicators. Do not talk about all of the indicators as you will only gain marks for two of them. You need to give detail to gain the marks. Remember, you need to explain why there is a difference between the UK and Chad.

Question	Expected answer	Mark	Commentary with hints and tips
12	**Advantages:** Mechanisation means less work for the farmer and it is quicker and more efficient (1). The use of fertilisers and pesticides increases crop yield (1) which leads to increased profit for the farmer (1) that can increase their standard of living (1). Increased yields allow a surplus to be produced encouraging trade to take place (1). The introduction of GM crops can give the farmer a more reliable harvest as the seeds are designed to resist disease (1). Crops can be grown in adverse conditions, e.g. lack of water, ensuring a better food supply for the people (1). The increased demand for biofuels can result in higher crop prices, improving the farmer's income and producing jobs (1). **Disadvantages:** Mechanisation can result in unemployment as machines do the work previously done by humans (1). Machinery is expensive and not all farmers can afford it, so they find it difficult to compete with those that have it (1). Increased use of fertilisers and pesticides can damage the environment if they get into the water (1). GM seeds do not always taste good (1).	6	Do not just describe the changes. Give the impact on the farmer as well.

Section 3: Global issues

Question	Expected answer	Mark	Commentary with hints and tips
13a	Overall greenhouse gas emissions increased between 1995 and 2015 (1). However, there was a decrease in both agriculture and buildings (1). The largest decrease was agriculture which dropped from 27% to 21%, a difference of 6% (1). Emissions increased in industry by 2% from 19% to 21% (1). Energy emissions increased the most from 32% to 37%, a rise of 5% (1). Emissions from buildings showed a small decrease of 1% (1).	4	In this question, you must use figures to gain full marks. General statements like higher or lower/increasing or decreasing might only gain you 2 marks. Try to process the information in some way. Since the question asks about changes, you would gain no marks for mentioning transport as there is no change in this category.
13b	Laws can be introduced to reduce the burning of forests, thus reducing the amount of CO_2 going into the atmosphere (1). Introducing replanting schemes where forests have been destroyed can reduce the amount of CO_2 in the atmosphere (1). The use of sprays that include CFCs can be reduced/banned as CFCs pollute the atmosphere (1). Council by-laws put in place to prevent illegal disposal of fridges, etc., so that no CFCs are allowed to escape (1). They can also introduce controlled disposal on waste dumping sites (1). Exhaust emissions containing lead and carbon dioxide can be reduced by adding filter systems to vehicle exhaust systems (1) and cars/lorries can be produced which use lead-free fuel (1). We can reduce the use of fossil fuels such as coal, oil and natural gases by introducing environmentally friendly fuels such as HEP, wind power, solar power and other renewable energy sources (1).	6	In this question, you need to give ways to manage climate change. You should put as much detail into your answer as possible. A simple list of methods will gain you only a few marks. Remember, this question is worth 6 marks so you need to make at least six valid points to get all of the marks.

Question	Expected answer	Mark	Commentary with hints and tips
14a	Overall the percentage of ice cover increased from 70% in 2000 to 92% in 2015 (1). Ice coverage increased slowly between 2000 and 2002, by 3% (1). It then dropped between 2002 and 2006 from 73% to 53%, a difference of 20% (1). The biggest drop was between 2009 and 2010 when it fell by 35% (1). It rose again between 2010 and 2012, reaching 89% in 2012 (1). It fell again in 2013 before reaching its highest point in 2015 at around 92% (1).	4	In this question, you must use figures and dates to gain full marks. General statements like higher or lower/ increasing or decreasing might only gain you 2 marks. Try to process the information in some way. Marks can be awarded for overall trends.
14b	**If the rainforest is chosen:** In Brazil, large areas have been cleared by timber companies and the hardwood has been exported abroad, earning income for the country (1) as well as providing jobs for the locals (1). Forests are cleared for new farmland, settlement and to increase food production, so destroying the habitats of wildlife (1). Burning trees releases vast quantities of carbon dioxide into the atmosphere and may contribute to global warming (1). The homes of indigenous tribes are destroyed, as is their traditional culture and way of life (1), and the people catch diseases from new settlers, causing many to die (1). Plants which may contain cures for diseases are also destroyed (1). When the trees have been cleared, there is less protection for the soil and heavy rain can lead to rapid soil erosion (1). Minerals are leached out of the soil and the soil quickly becomes infertile and useless (1). Poor farmers lose their land and may be forced to migrate to towns and cities to find employment, resulting in an increase in shanty towns (1). **If the tundra is chosen:** The discovery of oil in Alaska resulted in the building of the Trans-Alaska Pipeline that caused damage to the tundra vegetation and wildlife (1). The pipeline disrupts the habitat of the caribou, diverting them from their natural hunting areas and migration routes (1). Burst pipes have leaked hundreds of thousands of gallons of crude oil in Alaska, devastating the fragile environment (1). Oil spills from tankers like the *Exxon Valdez* have also been responsible for pollution in the region as well as causing the deaths of multitudes of birds and sea creatures (1). Local Inuit people have had their way of life disrupted as they must detour around the pipeline (1) and may no longer have access to their traditional hunting grounds (1). Some jobs were created by the oil industry, but few of them are available for locals and those jobs are poorly paid (1). Roads are built to transport workers and machinery, further damaging the vegetation and environment as well as creating air and noise pollution (1). The roads, however, improve access for the local people (1).	6	To gain full marks for this question, you need to mention both the people and the environment. Remember that you can mention both positive and negative effects in your answer. You should refer to specific case studies in your answer. Remember, the more detail in your answer, the more marks you can achieve. A list of effects will gain you only 1 mark. If you describe instead of explaining, you may get no marks at all.

Question	Expected answer	Mark	Commentary with hints and tips
15a	Active volcanoes are found along the edges of the plate boundaries (1). There is a large concentration around the Pacific Ring of Fire (1). There are a large number down the west coast of the USA and Alaska (1). The majority of volcanoes in South America are found down the west coast, for example in Chile (1). Europe has few volcanoes with most found around southern Europe, for example Mount Etna in Sicily (1). Any volcanoes in Africa are found on the eastern side of the continent with concentrations like the East African Rift Valley (1).	4	Remember that the map is there to help you answer the question. Try to name areas or countries in your answer. There are no marks for explanation, only for description, so do not explain your answer. Do not list places as this will gain you only 1 mark.
15b	**If the Japanese earthquake 2011 is chosen:** People living in earthquake prone areas like Japan have emergency plans in place so that they know exactly what to do during an earthquake (1). Emergency supplies such as bottled water and tinned food are stockpiled to ensure they have vital supplies to survive in the event of an earthquake (1). In Japanese schools, earthquake drills are held so that children know what to do if an earthquake occurs (1). Earthquake-resistant buildings reduce the number of people trapped or killed, as the buildings are designed to twist and sway instead of collapsing (1). Sprinkler systems and gas cut-off valves prevent fires spreading, reducing the number of people injured and buildings destroyed (1). The government sends texts and issues warnings on TV giving the people some warning to evacuate or take cover (1). The government has plans in place to allow aid to be sent to an affected area quickly, thus reducing the number of injured (1).	6	Do not list the strategies as this will gain you only 1 mark. The question asks for explanation so you must give reasons in your answer. State the strategy, then say why it reduces the effects. Avoid describing. You need to refer to an example you have studied otherwise you may lose a mark.
16a	Overall the percentage volume of world trade has decreased since 2008 (1). It dropped steeply between 2008 and 2009 from +6% to −18% (1), a drop of 24% (1). It then rose steeply between 2009 and 2010 from −18% to +19% (1), an increase of 37% (1). It reached its highest point in 2010 at +19% (1). It then steadily decreased till 2013 where it remained relatively steady until 2014 (1). It continued to drop to around 1% in 2015 (1).	4	In this question, you must use figures and dates to gain full marks. General statements like higher or lower/increasing or decreasing might only gain you 2 marks. Try to process the information in some way. Marks can be awarded for overall trends.

Question	Expected answer	Mark	Commentary with hints and tips
16b	Developed countries have a larger share of world trade because their exports include a lot more manufactured goods than countries in the developing world (1). Developing countries tend to produce raw materials rather than manufactured goods (1), and manufactured goods sell for more than raw materials (1). Developed countries have more industries producing a wide variety of products which are traded with other developed countries (1). Many developed countries like Germany belong to trading alliances such as the European Union, which help to increase the volume of trade (1). The economies of developed countries benefit from being able to purchase low-cost raw materials produced by developing countries and sell manufactured goods back for higher profits (1). Developing countries like Chad have much less money to invest in manufacturing industries and are less able to compete with developed countries (1).	6	Try to give examples in your answer. In some cases, if you do not give an example or refer to a case study, you can lose a mark. Remember, this is an explanation question so you need to give reasons in your answer.
17a	International tourist arrivals increased in all of these areas (1). The greatest increase was in Asia and the Pacific which more than quadrupled (1), increasing by 209 million in 24 years (1). Europe more than doubled (1), increasing from 250 million in 1990 to 575 million in 2014, an increase of 325 million (1). The Americas nearly doubled from 99 million to 189 million, an increase of 90 million (1). In 2009 all three areas saw a decrease in arrivals (1) with Europe decreasing by 31 million (1).	4	In this question, you must use figures and dates to gain full marks. General statements like higher or lower/ increasing or decreasing might only gain you 2 marks. Try to process the information in some way. Marks can be awarded for overall trends.

Question	Expected answer	Mark	Commentary with hints and tips
17b	In Mallorca, mass tourism creates employment for the local people in shops, hotels, restaurants, car hire, etc. (1). It decreases unemployment and increases the standards of living (1). The income from tourism allows the government to improve infrastructure, e.g. transport, water supplies and sewage systems (1). The facilities provided for the tourists can be used by the locals, improving their access to sports facilities, clubs and water parks (1). An increased demand for food to supply hotels, restaurants and cafes provides farmers with a larger market for their produce, increasing their profit (1). However, employment can be seasonal as many hotels in resorts like Pollensa close at the end of October (1). Traditional ways of life can be lost as young people leave the countryside to live and work in the tourist resorts rather than on family farms (2). Tourism creates pollution, e.g. litter on beaches (1). Increased traffic causes noise and air pollution as well as traffic congestion in local villages (2). Large numbers of tourists visiting natural features like limestone caves can damage the delicate structures (1). Beaches are eroded as sand is carried away on tourists' feet (1). Large areas of natural grassland/forest are removed to make way for new hotels, etc. (1), destroying the natural habitat of plants and animals (1).	6	For full marks, you need to mention both the people and the environment. You should refer to examples you have studied. The question asks for the impact of mass tourism. Remember, that means you can mention both advantages and disadvantages in your answer.
18a	Areas like North America, Australasia and Europe have health-care access of over 95% (1). The area with the least health-care access is Africa with many countries having less than 20% (1). The only country in southern Africa with health-care access over 95% is South Africa (1). Most African countries that border the Mediterranean Sea have over 50% health care, with Libya having over 95% (1). The only country in Africa bordering the Mediterranean which has less is Morocco at between 20% and 49% (1). Most of South America has over 50% health-care access apart from Paraguay, Bolivia and Ecuador (1). India is the main area in Asia with less than 20% (1).	4	Remember, the map is there for you to use to answer the question. Try to name areas or countries in your answer, as well as referring to percentages. There are no marks for explanation, only for description, so do not explain your answer. Do not list places as this will gain you only 1 mark.
18b	Health education programmes have been introduced to limit the spread of HIV/AIDS in developing and developed countries (1) promoting the benefits of safe sex and the dangers of sharing hypodermic needles (1). Antiretroviral drugs, which work by stopping the virus replicating in the body, allowing the immune system to repair itself and preventing further damage, are more freely available (1). Condoms are available for free (1) and TV and radio advertising has been used to inform the public (1). Agencies such as the World Bank have made funding available to developing countries to tackle the disease (1). In developed countries, needle exchanges and drug therapy programmes have been introduced (1).	6	Do not simply list the strategies. You should add as much detail to your answer as possible. Refer to examples if you can.

Practice Paper 2

Section 1: Physical environments

Question	Expected answer	Mark	Commentary with hints and tips
1a	Headland: 570863 Stack: 612869 Bay: 535877	3	First match the features you are sure are correct. You can then match any remaining feature to its reference. Do not leave a feature without a reference. Even if you do not know the correct answer, make a guess at the remaining references as you could be lucky and match them correctly!
1b	 (a) Beginning of Ice Age (b) During Ice Age (c) After Ice Age Snow accumulates in a north-facing hollow in a mountainside where the snow becomes compacted and turns into ice (1); the glacier moves downhill due to gravity (1). Plucking occurs on the back wall, making it steeper (1). The ice sticks to the sides and pulls pieces of rock away as it moves (1). Abrasion deepens the bottom of the hollow (1) as rock fragments embedded in the bottom of the glacier act like sandpaper, wearing away the land (1). When temperatures rose at the end of the Ice Age, the glacier melted, leaving behind an armchair-shaped hollow with steep sides (1). A rock lip forms at the edge of the hollow and water becomes trapped, creating a corrie lake or tarn (1).	4	The more detail you put into an answer, the more marks you will gain. If you simply refer to glacial processes like plucking, abrasion and freeze-thaw, you will gain only 1 mark. However, you will gain additional marks if you explain the processes. You can gain a mark for drawing a series of diagrams that show how the feature is formed at different stages. A diagram with labels which explain the formation can gain full marks.

Question	Expected answer	Mark	Commentary with hints and tips
2a	V-shaped valley: 652516 Meander: 591515 Waterfall: 575535	3	First match the features you are sure are correct. You can then match any remaining feature to its reference. Do not leave a feature without a reference. Even if you do not know the correct answer, make a guess at the remaining references as you could be lucky and match it correctly!
2b	In the upper course, the water flows naturally downhill eroding the landscape vertically (1). The river erodes a deep groove into the landscape using hydraulic action, corrasion and corrosion. As the river erodes downwards, the sides of the valley are exposed to weathering which loosens the rocks and steepens the valley sides (1). The rocks which fall into the river help with the process of corrasion, which leads to further erosion (1). The river transports the rocks downstream (1) and the channel becomes wider and deeper, creating a V-shaped valley between interlocking spurs (1).	4	The more detail you put into an answer, the more marks you will gain. You should mention processes in your answer. A list of processes like hydraulic action and corrosion will gain you just 1 mark. A detailed explanation of the processes will gain you more marks. You can gain a mark from drawing a series of diagrams which show how the feature is formed at different stages. A diagram with labels which explain the formation can gain full marks.
3	The low-lying flat land has encouraged the growth of settlements such as Swansea and Llanelli (5300) as it is suitable for building on (1). Due to its coastal location, it has allowed the development of docks at 672927 (1) enabling trade to take place (1). Communication links, for example the vehicle ferry to Cork at 665924, have developed because of its coastal location (1). Roads like the A406 have followed the natural route created by the River Afon Tawe (1). The marshland found along the river estuary, for example at 5496, has prevented any building in that area (1). The coastal area has encouraged the growth of tourism with many car parks and caravan/campsites around Oxwich Bay (5186) (1). The flat low-lying land has encouraged arable farming to take place as the flat land allows machinery to be used (1).	6	This question is about how the physical landscape affects the land use. Make sure you do not simply describe the land use on the map. You need to identify a feature of the landscape from the map, then say what it is used for and why. For example: 'Feature of the landscape is flat land, identified land use – settlement – flat land good for building on.' You should also try to give a grid reference to identify the location you are discussing. In some questions 1 mark is available for a grid reference, and this should be preferably a six-figure grid reference at National 5.
4	**Advantages:** This air mass can bring snowy conditions, which allows people to take part in outdoor activities like sledging and skiing (1). Increasing sales of winter goods such as hats, gloves and sledges increase shop profits (1). Ski resort bookings will increase, bringing more money to the local economy (1). **Disadvantages:** More accidents due to the slippery conditions result in people being admitted to hospital with broken limbs, etc. (1). This puts an extra strain on the health service (1). Additional supplies of electricity are needed as people turn up their central heating to keep warm, putting pressure on the National Grid (2). Increased use of electricity means people have to find additional money to pay for higher bills (1). Freezing temperatures can cause pipes to burst causing water damage to homes (1). Travel is disrupted, affecting business as workers cannot reach their employment (1).	4	You must give at least one advantage and one disadvantage in your answer. You should make at least four points in total to receive maximum marks.

Question	Expected answer	Mark	Commentary with hints and tips
5a	The temperature in set B is 11 degrees higher than in set A (1). There is twice as much cloud cover at 8 oktas in set A than in set B (1). There is heavy rain in set A but showers in set B (1). There is a lot less wind in set B than in set A, by 30 knots (1).	3	Take each element and say something about the differences between the station circles.
5b	Set A is correct for Birmingham (1). There is heavy rain in Birmingham because there is a cold front over Birmingham (1). The isobars are close together so wind speeds are high (1). There are heavy cumulonimbus clouds present in a cold front so 8 oktas would be correct (1). The wind direction is SW, which is correct as the wind follows the direction of the isobars (1).	5	You can say what is correct or incorrect about both station circles.
6	**If upland limestone landscape is chosen:** **Farming and industry** Areas of the Yorkshire Dales are used to quarry limestone, and blasting to remove the rock can disturb farm animals (1) as well as cause sheep to miscarry their lambs (1). Large, heavy lorries are used to transport the limestone blocks along the small country roads, hampering farmers when moving animals, equipment and products (1). The blasting produces dust which can lie on the fields affecting crop growth (1). The streams in the area can get polluted when the dust is washed into them making them unsuitable for animals to drink (1). Other examples could be as follows. **If industry and recreation/tourism is chosen:** Tourists/visitors may be restricted from visiting certain areas (1). Noise from military operations may disturb visitors (1). Military vehicles and tourist traffic may result in serious traffic congestion (1). **If recreation/tourism and farming is chosen:** Walkers with dogs may worry sheep and cause them to miscarry (1) affecting the income of the farmer (1). Tourists leave gates open allowing animals to escape (1), and they drop litter which animals may eat (1). Farmers may restrict access across their land (1).	5	Read the question carefully. You must identify the landscape you are talking about in your answer or you may lose a mark. If you are asked for two land uses, then you only need to write about how your two chosen land uses conflict and not all of them. This answer gives three examples of conflicts between different types of land uses. You only need to choose two.

Section 2: Human environments

Question	Expected answer	Mark	Commentary with hints and tips
7a	The main transport links meet in this square (1). There is a bus station (1) and there is a train station (1). There are several churches (1) and a town hall (1).	3	Make sure you give actual map evidence. Do not use generic points in your answer.
7b	These developments like Kelvin Industrial Estate at 640525 are located on the edge of East Kilbride so land will be cheaper (1). There is space for expansion to the south of the industrial estate (1). There are housing areas like Whitehills close by at 635524 which can supply a labour force (1) as well as a market for its products (1). The A725 runs close by allowing goods to be transported in and out of the area (1).	5	This question must be answered using map evidence. You need to give reasons for the location of these businesses on the edge of town. You need to give explanations, not just description. For example, instead of saying there is a road nearby (description) you should say there is a road nearby, the A725, which allows goods to be transported in and out. Since this is a map question, you should try to use grid references, preferably a six-figure reference, in your answer.
8	There is flat land to easily build the houses on (1). The land on the rural/urban fringe is cheaper, so low-density housing with gardens/garages can be built (1). The A723 is close by (1) which people can use to commute to their workplaces (1). There is also a train station and a bus station in Hamilton allowing travel further afield (1). The area is on the edge of the town, so there will be less noise and air pollution (1) and less traffic, so it will be safer for families (1). There are woods nearby, where residents can go for walks to relax (1). Calderglen Country Park and Strathclyde Loch are also close by so residents can pursue outdoor activities (1).	5	Avoid a list. Describe the map evidence, then say why it is good for building houses.
9	Sparsely populated areas like deserts are too dry to allow crops to grow so they can support only a limited population (1). In the tundra areas of North America, the extreme cold means that the ground is permanently frozen below one metre, so the permafrost makes the building of houses and roads difficult (1). It also means there is a short growing season, which prevents the growth of crops, so food has to be flown in, making it expensive to live there (1). In areas such as the UK, there is a moderate climate with enough rainfall to provide a reliable source of drinking water (1). Rainforests have a low population density as they are uncomfortable to live in due to the humid climate (1), and diseases like malaria spread easily (1). People avoid living in mountainous areas like the Himalayas as they are difficult to access (1) and difficult to build on as machinery cannot be used (1). Coastal areas allow trade to take place so ports and industries develop, encouraging people to live nearby as they provide jobs (1). Upland areas are cold and wet, which makes it difficult to grow crops, so few people live there (1). Many people tend to live in areas where there are minerals and raw materials to extract and sell (1).	6	Avoid a simple list of points. Give a reason why people live or do not live in that area.

Question	Expected answer	Mark	Commentary with hints and tips
10	**If Kibera, Nairobi is chosen:** New roads are to be constructed to improve the transport of people and goods in the area (1). Storm drains are to be built to control flooding (1). Construction of piped water supply into the shanty town (1) to reduce the chance of waterborne diseases like cholera (1). Construction of latrines to stop sewage contaminating the streets (1). Slums will be cleared over a five-year period (1) and people are being rehoused nearby in newly built apartments (1). This is affordable accommodation and the estates also include schools, markets and other facilities (1).	5	You must use a specific example in your answer. You should put as much detail into your answer as possible.
11	In stage 3, the death rate continues to fall due to continued improvements in medicine (1) and increased standards of living (1). The birth rate falls rapidly with the growth of family planning (1), and smaller families are needed as fewer babies die (1). Population grows rapidly at the beginning of stage 3 due to the differences in the birth and death rates (1), but growth levels off at the end of stage 3 as the birth rate and death rate reach similar low levels (1). In stage 4, a decreasing birth rate is shown with people wanting smaller (cheaper) families (1), women following careers, greater access to family planning (contraception/abortion) (2), a decreasing death rate and increasing life expectancy due to improved health care, sanitation, housing, food supply (2), pensions and care for the elderly (1). Low birth rates and low death rates mean very low population growth (1).	6	This question asks for explanation so you need to give reasons in your answer. Description of stages 3 and 4 will get few if any marks. Make sure you refer to both stages in your answer.

Section 3: Global issues

Question	Expected answer	Mark	Commentary with hints and tips
12a	The percentage of energy from fossil fuels will decrease from 78% in 2009 to 52% in 2020 (1). Gas will decrease the most, falling from 45% to 29% (1) a difference of 16% (1), whereas coal will fall by 10% (1). Nuclear power will also decrease by 5% (1). Renewable energy will increase from 6% to 31% (1), a difference of 25% (1).	4	In this question, you must use figures to gain full marks. General statements like higher or lower/ increasing or decreasing might only gain you 2 marks. Do not describe one pie chart followed by the other. The question asks for differences so process the information you are given in some way. You could also mention trends in your answer.
12b	Increased temperatures are causing ice caps to melt so the habitats of animals like the polar bear are beginning to disappear (1). Melting ice causes sea levels to rise (1), threatening coastal settlements like Bangladesh and the Netherlands (1). Climate change could also affect weather patterns, leading to more droughts in areas of Africa (1) and more flooding in areas of the UK (1). In the UK, some crops such as seed potatoes may not grow as well because of warmer and wetter conditions (1) but farmers may be able to grow different crops such as soft fruit in their place (1). Some fish species may move further north, affecting the livelihoods of those in the fishing industry in the UK (1).	6	Remember not to describe or list the effects. You need to explain the effects. To gain full marks, you need to mention the effects on both people and the environment as well as mentioning both local and global effects.

Question	Expected answer	Mark	Commentary with hints and tips
13a	Between 2001 and 2014, the overall trend was a decrease in tree loss (1). The years with the greatest tree loss were 2004 and 2005 (1) with 2.5 million hectares lost in 2004 and 2.4 million lost in 2005 (1). Tree loss decreased between 2005 and 2009 from 2.4 million hectares to 1 million hectares (1), a decrease of 1.4 million hectares (1). It then rose by 0.4 million in 2010 (1) before falling once again by just under 0.4 million in 2011 (1). It rose to 1.4 million in 2012 before falling once again to 1 million hectares in 2013 (1). The trend is upwards again in 2014 increasing by 0.1 million (1).	4	In this question, you must use figures to gain full marks. General statements like higher or lower/ increasing or decreasing might only gain you 2 marks.
13b	**Fires, mining, urbanisation, road construction and dams:** Large areas of the world's rainforest are destroyed every year by the deliberate burning of trees to create land for other uses, contributing to the greenhouse effect (1) as well as altering the local climate (1). Mining washes away the topsoil, destroying the growing environment of the trees (1). Rivers are severely polluted, causing further damage to the forest environment as well as making the water undrinkable for the indigenous people (1). Trees are removed to create space for major highways, such as the Trans-Amazonian Highway, but this destroys the local habitat of plants and animals (1). Huge areas of rainforest are flooded when dams are built in order to create hydroelectric plants but they flood large areas of rainforest, forcing the indigenous people to move away from their traditional hunting areas (1). Settlements are built on the edge of the forest, destroying the natural habitat (1). **Logging:** Trees are cut down both legally and illegally, reducing the biodiversity of the forest (1). Animal habitats are destroyed and some animals could become extinct (1). The logging operations destroy areas around the logged area, removing plants which could provide cures for diseases (1).	6	The question asks for an explanation, so make sure you do not just describe the land uses. Say what the land use is, then say why it causes deforestation. Make sure you make enough points to gain 6 marks. Refer to specific examples you have studied as this adds detail to your answer.
14a	Earthquakes occur along or near the plate boundaries (1) in southern Europe, through the Middle East and into eastern and South East Asia (1). There are also earthquakes stretching from Alaska down through the west coast of the USA, through Mexico and down the west coast of South America (1). The main concentration of earthquakes is around the Pacific Ring of Fire (1). There is a large concentration around the Indonesian islands (1). There are some located in the north of India and the Himalayas (1). In Africa, most are located on the eastern side of the continent (1).	4	Remember, the map is there to help you answer the question. Try to name areas or countries in your answer. There are no marks for explanation, only for description, so do not explain your answer. Do not list places as this will gain you only 1 mark.

Question	Expected answer	Mark	Commentary with hints and tips
14b	**If earthquakes are chosen, answers may include:** In Japan, earthquake drills are held so that people are aware of what to do in an earthquake (1). Warning systems are put in place in order to give people some time to evacuate or move to a safer area (1), e.g. in Japan the government send warning texts and broadcast warnings on TV (1). Earthquake-resistant buildings are built with deep foundations, shock absorbers and reinforced concrete (1). The buildings are designed to sway instead of collapsing so reducing the number of deaths and injuries (1). Apartment buildings in Tokyo have sprinkler systems and gas cut-off valves to prevent fires spreading (1). Earthquake survival kits containing bottled water, tinned food and torches are put together, allowing people to survive until they are rescued (1). Sea walls are built in coastal areas to protect the coastline from tsunamis resulting from earthquakes at sea (1). **If tropical storms are chosen, answers may include:** In Hurricane Katrina, satellite images provided advance warning allowing the population time to evacuate New Orleans (1) and protect buildings by boarding up windows and doors (1). Public buildings were opened to provide people with shelter from the storm (1). People could prepare to protect themselves by building storm shelters under the ground (1). Storm warnings were given over the radio and television (1). Local people could stock up on food and water supplies to use until the storm had passed (1). Local evacuation routes were well signposted, ensuring people knew where to go if evacuation was necessary (1).	6	Do not list as this will gain you only 1 mark. The question asks for explanation, so you must give reasons in your answer. State the method, then say why it reduces the effects. Avoid describing. You need to refer to an example you have studied otherwise you may lose a mark. Examples are given for tropical storms and earthquakes. You only need to answer on one disaster.
15a	The United States share of GDP changed from 29.7% in 2003 to 22.2% in 2013 (1) a drop of 7.5% in ten years (1). The EU had the largest share of world trade in both 2003 and 2013, but this share dropped 7% from 30.7% to 23.7% in 2013 (1). China's share nearly tripled from 4.3% in 2003 to 12.1% in 2013 (1), a rise of 7.8% (1). The rest of the world's share increased by 4.9% (1). Canada and Mexico are no longer present in 2013 and are replaced by Russia and Brazil (1).	4	In this question, you must use figures to gain full marks. General statements like higher or lower/ increasing or decreasing might only gain you 2 marks.
15b	Ghana depends on cocoa for 85% of its exports and if the price of cocoa were to fall, cocoa farmers would receive less income (1). They would have less to spend, affecting other businesses in Ghana (1). They can find themselves with nothing to trade (1) and they are then forced to borrow money and end up in debt (1). They then may have to borrow money to pay the debt, limiting their chances for development (1) and the chance to trade in higher-priced manufactured goods (1). If the price of the export in a developing country were to increase then there would be more income for the country to invest in other products and industries (1). Countries would be less affected if they had a greater range of products to export (1) and this could lead to improvements in infrastructure, education and health.	6	This question asks for explanation so make sure you give reasons in your answer. Try to refer to an example/ country you have studied. The more detail you give, the more marks you will achieve. Remember, for 6 marks you should make six points.

Question	Expected answer	Mark	Commentary with hints and tips
16a	The number of tourist arrivals to Europe is expected to decrease from 50% to 41% (1), a drop of 9% (1). The greatest increase in tourist arrivals is in Asia and the Pacific, from 22% to 29% (1), a rise of 7% (1). The Americas have decreased by 3% (1). Both the Middle East and Africa have increased (1) with Africa slightly more and now equalling the Middle East (1).	4	In this question, you must use figures to gain full marks. General statements like higher or lower/ increasing or decreasing might only gain you 2 marks. Try to process the figures.
16b	Ecotourism, in countries such as South Africa, helps the people of a developing country by bringing more money into the economy (1). It provides financial benefits to local people (1), e.g. jobs as tour guides (1), and gives them some control over developments in their home area (1). Ecotourism aims to minimise the impact of tourism on an area (1). It promotes responsible travel to natural areas and conserves the environment (1). It raises awareness of the natural environment and the culture of the area (1). Some of the money raised from this type of tourism is used for conservation of the area and its people's way of life (1). Ecotourism tries to ensure that the tourists have a positive experience without negatively affecting the local people and the environment (1). Money from tourism helps to improve the local and natural environment by ensuring beaches remain clean, historic buildings and sites are maintained, and wildlife and safari parks are set up to protect the local wildlife (1).	6	Try to relate the question to an area you have studied. You may lose a mark if you do not refer to a named example. Mention examples in your answer. You should make reference to both the people and the environment.
17a	The main areas of obesity in the world with over 25% include the USA, Canada, Australia and New Zealand (1). In Europe, the main obese areas with over 25% are the UK, the Czech Republic and the island of Mallorca (1). In South America, there are no countries with over 25% (1) with most countries (including Brazil) having between 15% and 24.9% (1). Bolivia, Paraguay, Ecuador and Guyana have less obesity with 5% to 14.9% (1). In Africa, only Libya has more than 25% obesity (1). Many countries, including the Sahel zone as well as central and eastern Africa, have less than 5% obesity (1). The whole of India, Bangladesh and Pakistan are less than 5% (1).	4	At National 5, you are expected to know the names of the continents and some countries. This question lends itself to giving a list of countries. As long as you relate your list to the level of obesity as shown in the answer, this will be acceptable.
17b	**If heart disease is chosen:** Heart disease can be inherited from parents so predisposes a person to developing the disease (1). Over-eating can lead to obesity, putting extra pressure on the heart (1). Smoking narrows the arteries and affects the lungs (1). This can lead to a condition known as emphysema, putting a strain on the heart by making it work faster (1). The build-up of fatty deposits on the walls of the arteries restricts the flow of blood to the heart (1). Lack of exercise raises blood pressure, affecting the efficiency of the heart (1). Poor diet increases cholesterol which furs up and narrows the arteries (1). Stress leads to high blood pressure resulting in the heart having to work faster (1).	6	This question lends itself to a list. Try to avoid this. Try to expand your answer to explain the effect on the heart – for example 'over-eating' can be expanded into 'over-eating causes obesity, and the extra weight carried puts a strain on the heart'.

Have you seen our full range of revision and exam practice resources?

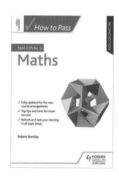